FREEDOM
FROM THE
RELIGIOUS
SPIRIT

C. PETER WAGNER

Regal

From Gospel Light
Ventura, California, U.S.A.

PUBLISHED BY REGAL BOOKS
FROM GOSPEL LIGHT
VENTURA, CALIFORNIA, U.S.A.
Regal PRINTED IN THE U.S.A.

Regal Books is a ministry of Gospel Light, a Christian publisher dedicated to serving the local church. We believe God's vision for Gospel Light is to provide church leaders with biblical, user-friendly materials that will help them evangelize, disciple and minister to children, youth and families.

It is our prayer that this Regal book will help you discover biblical truth for your own life and help you meet the needs of others. May God richly bless you.

For a free catalog of resources from Regal Books/Gospel Light, please call your Christian supplier or contact us at 1-800-4-GOSPEL *or* www.regalbooks.com.

Library of Congress Cataloging-in-Publication Data
Freedom from the religious spirit / C. Peter Wagner, editor.
    p. cm.
Includes bibliographical references.
ISBN 0-8307-3670-0 (trade pbk.)
    1. Devil—Christianity. 2. Spiritual warfare. 3. Church renewal. 4. Church growth.
5. Holy Spirit. I. Wagner, C. Peter.
    BT982.F74 2005
    241'.3—dc22   2005001115

2 3 4 5 6 7 8 9 10 11 12 13 14 15 / 11 10 09 08 07 06 05

Rights for publishing this book in other languages are contracted by Gospel Light Worldwide, the international nonprofit ministry of Gospel Light. Gospel Light Worldwide also provides publishing and technical assistance to international publishers dedicated to producing Sunday School and Vacation Bible School curricula and books in the languages of the world. For additional information, visit www.gospellightworldwide.org; write to Gospel Light Worldwide, P.O. Box 3875, Ventura, CA 93006; or send an e-mail to info@gospellightworldwide.org.

CONTENTS

FOREWORD

Life should be filled with joy. Nehemiah 8:10 reads, "The joy of the LORD is your strength." One of the great joys of my life has been to work alongside C. Peter Wagner. Peter is a man filled with joy. He enjoys life, people, ministry, his family, food and even his own jokes. He is full of joy, for one, because he never lets life get stale. I believe that a key to his life is *his love for embracing change*. When God decides it is time to bring change into the earthly realm through new thought processes, Peter seems to be one of the first on this earth to raise his hand and say, "Use me!" That is why he could write this book, *Freedom from the Religious Spirit*.

What is a religious spirit and how does it work? This book boldly explores and explains how this deceptive force has labored to stop the progress of the Church throughout the ages. Religion is not a bad thing when we adhere to the word's literal meaning: to consider divine things. The word "religion" has three meanings in the Word of God: outward religious acts, such as praying and going to church; the feeling of absolute dependence; and the observance of moral law as a divine institution. James 1:26-27 defines "religion" from the Christian point of view: "If anyone among you thinks he is religious, and does not bridle his tongue but deceives his own heart, this one's religion is useless. Pure and undefiled religion before God and the Father is this: to visit orphans and widows in their trouble, and to keep oneself unspotted from the world."

Religion is linked with worship. Religion, when pure, is very powerful. However, religion is also defined as an organized system of doctrine with an approved pattern of behavior. Behavior has to demonstrate a proper form of worship. This is where we move from pure and undefiled religion to ritual. Demons of doctrine rob individuals of their freedom to worship a holy God in purity by instituting rules and regulations for their worship.

I have always been a creative thinker and an expressive worshiper. I have been known throughout the Body of Christ as a modern-day prophet who expresses the heart and mind of God, and I have always had to maneuver past spirits of religion that would resist this gift of God. Demons hate revelation from God. They resist those gifts in the Body that bring revelatory freedom to the members of the Body. They attempt to stone the revelation of apostles and prophets, because this revealed word establishes God's foundation in the Church for this age. First Corinthians 12:28 sets an order of governmental gifts in the Church for victory in the world. That order is "first apostles, second prophets." Religious spirits attempt to defy God's order.

Religious spirits can also just deny change! Our minds and processes of thought aid the Spirit of God to produce change in the earth, but the carnal mind is in enmity with God. Religious spirits attempt to block strategic thinking for the future. They can make individuals get so routinized, or in a rut, that they do not want to shift into today's methods for victory.

In the New Testament, the Lord's disciples had to have revelation of who He was, who they were and who their enemy was. The Pharisees had a choice either to deny the divine nature of God's Son or to align themselves with Him. They had to choose either to keep rules in place that prevented any behavioral change in worship or to begin to worship in Spirit and truth. Most failed in making the choice that could have changed their lives, their families and their society. Therefore, in Matthew 16:18-19 we find Jesus taking the keys of the kingdom of heaven from the scribes and Pharisees and giving them to the future leaders who would defy religion and lead the Church into its future. The same is true today. We must know who Christ is, who we are and who our enemy is, and we must choose to follow the Spirit as He leads us into these days of transformation.

Romans 12:2 reads, "Do not be conformed to this world, but be transformed by the renewing of your mind, that you may prove what is that good and acceptable and perfect will of God." The word "transform" means to change, transfigure or experience a metamorphosis, such as a caterpillar, which is transformed into a butterfly. The Lord told His people, Israel, that they could change from being worms to being new, sharp instruments with teeth that would thresh the mountains (see Isa. 41:14-16). However, prior to giving this promise of transformation, the Lord says, "Fear not" (v. 14).

In compiling *Freedom from the Religious Spirit*, Peter Wagner has gathered a wonderful team of contributors around him. The truths contained in this book unlock revelation for today and release keys. I want to encourage you, as you read this book, "Fear not." Fear not change! Fear not embracing the paradigms that need to be expressed today to bring change. Fear not confrontation. Fear not the next great move of the Spirit of God. Fear not letting go of worship methods in the Church that have caused us to become comfortable. Defy the spirits of religion around you and move with boldness into your future!

Chuck D. Pierce
Vice President, Global Harvest Ministries
President, Glory of Zion International Ministries, Inc.

GETTING STARTED

I would guess that I have heard the term "the spirit of religion" mentioned in sermons about a thousand times. But as I think back, I cannot remember a whole teaching on the subject from the Christian leaders whom I know. That is, until recently.

I heard the first message on the spirit of religion no earlier than 2003, and then, surprisingly, I heard two more the same year. My antennae went on high alert, for it was only a year earlier, namely in 2002, that I sensed God speaking to me personally about giving some priority to researching and writing on the spirit of religion. As I have been undertaking this, I have discovered both that it is an extremely important issue and that it is quite a bit deeper an area than many may have imagined.

This religious spirit is not just an attitude of religiosity. It is actually an evil spirit that must be resisted, bound and cast out. I will describe this spirit in more detail later.

I am including this short introductory chapter in an attempt to get us all on the same page before we dive into the details. I am extremely excited about this book and about the revelation that it will bring to the Body of Christ.

THE LARGE PICTURE

Realizing that what I have learned about the spirit of religion since 2002 is only a fraction of the large picture that needs to come together, I began contacting some of my friends who also have logged time and experience in attempting to understand more about this subject. The result of this is a lineup of knowledgeable Christian leaders who not only reference and renounce the spirit of religion in sermons and writings but who also have gone much deeper through thoughtful analysis. When you read the chapters of this book, you will be amazed by what you find. The Body of Christ will begin to know much more than ever before about how this agent of darkness has been deceiving both Christians and non-Christians.

Some people will ask why we would do this, why we would want to know more about a high-ranking demon. It is very simple. As Paul writes, "Lest Satan should take advantage of us; for we are not ignorant of his devices" (2 Cor. 2:11). Turn this around, and it means that if for any reason, we *are* ignorant of the devices or the wiles of the devil, he will inevitably take advantage of us! I am convinced that the spirit of religion is one of the most clever agents of Satan. It is a master of deception. I believe that this pernicious spirit has succeeded in keeping most of us ignorant of its devices through the years, and therefore it has taken advantage of us, as the Bible says it would. I hope that this book helps put a stop to it once and for all.

I will introduce each of my friends who have joined me in this project at the beginning of the chapter that he or she has written, so I do not need to do it now. But we all fully believe that we are poised to deal a severe blow that will set back the intentions of Satan. We believe that we are accurately hearing the Spirit of God saying, "Enough is enough!" Now is the time to expose these wiles of the devil!

This book will prove to be very exciting reading for all those who are committed to seeing the kingdom of God advance aggressively in this season. I believe it will help us be transformed by the renewing of our minds, as Paul would say (see

Rom. 12:2). If you go through this material and allow the Holy
Spirit to apply it to you personally, to your family, to your
church and to your community, you will never be the same!

C. Peter Wagner

Chapter One

THE CORPORATE SPIRIT OF RELIGION

C. PETER WAGNER

C. Peter Wagner is widely recognized as a leading authority in the fields of church growth and spiritual warfare. Wagner is cofounder of the World Prayer Center and is chancellor of the Wagner Institute in Colorado Springs, Colorado. He is the author of Changing Church *and* Your Spiritual Gifts Can Help Your Church Grow.

WHAT DO WE KNOW?

What do we, as the Body of Christ, currently know about the spirit of religion?

Frankly, I don't think that we know very much. We know that it is bad. We know that we don't like it. We know that we must break it or bind it. We know that we must warn others against it. But we don't know much else.

One of our problems is that "spirit of religion" is not a biblical term. You can't find it in the concordance. That does not imply, of course, that it is not a useful term. When you think of it, you can't find "Trinity" or "abortion" or "Christmas" in the concordance either, just to cite a few examples, but they are good words that we frequently use. Even the word "religion," by itself, appears only two times in the Bible. Once it refers to Judaism (see Acts 26:5) and the other simply tells us that true religion, like true faith, is accompanied by works (see Jas. 1:26-27).

Because of this shortage of explicit biblical information on the spirit of religion, we must depend, more than with some other subjects, on seeking God's fresh revelation. If the Spirit is saying to the churches that we must increase our awareness of the spirit of religion, which I believe He is, God will supernaturally show us the direction we need to take.

A DEFINITION OF "THE SPIRIT OF RELIGION"

It is good to start out with a working definition, so I'll suggest one. As I have studied this for some time now, I have come to the conclusion that *the spirit of religion is an agent of Satan assigned to prevent change and to maintain the status quo by using religious devices.*[1]

Many people use the term "religious spirit" as a synonym for "the spirit of religion," and the terms are used interchangeably in this book. I am aware that some argue that there should be a technical distinction between the two, and they may be right. However I have chosen to take the more simplified approach, at least for the moment.

I'm using the terms "religion" and "religious" in the common sense of the words, namely beliefs and activities involved in relating to superhuman or supernatural beings or forces.

Knowing what we already know about the invisible world of darkness from what we read in Scripture, we can safely surmise certain things. For example, there certainly must be *many* spirits of religion, not just one. Consequently, our term "the spirit of religion" should be understood as a generic term, embracing however many of these demons there might actually be.

Now, in order to paint the big picture, I am going to use my imagination a bit. In doing so, I want to identify with Paul, who said at one point concerning a certain matter that "I have no commandment from the Lord; yet I give judgment as one whom the Lord in His mercy has made trustworthy" (1 Cor. 7:25). The other authors in this book and I certainly are not writing about the spirit of religion with the authority of biblical revelation, yet we do believe that we have clearly heard from the Lord on the matter. With that disclaimer, here then is my hypothesis. I want it to be seen as my personal attempt to explain a rather complex state of affairs in as simple language as possible.

THE LUCIFERIAN DEPARTMENT OF RELIGION

Let's imagine that Satan's kingdom has something like a Luciferian Department of Religion and that there are two major divisions of that department: the Division of Non-Christian Religions and the Division of Christendom.

Let me explain.

The Division of Non-Christian Religions

One of the devices that Satan uses to keep unsaved people from being saved is the spirit of religion. The issue for this religious spirit, which is in charge of controlling the Division of Non-Christian Religions, would be allegiance. In other words, the spirit is concerned about to whom a particular individual or a group gives allegiance. Keep in mind that the spirit of religion most of the time attempts to preserve the status quo. In this case, it uses religion to keep people from switching their allegiance to Jesus Christ. That is to say, it devises strategies to keep Moroccans committed to Allah or Japanese committed to the Sun Goddess or Thai people committed to Buddha or the Aymaras of the Andes committed to Inti, just to choose a few random examples.

The Division of Christendom

Let's also assume that there are two offices in the Division of Christendom.

The first office could be an Office of Personal Religious Security. The religious spirit overseeing this office would primarily target individuals; its central issues are either salvation or fullness. The spirit of religion's primary strategy here is to promote the idea that belonging to a Christian church or doing religious things is what saves you. It succeeds if it can, for example, persuade Catholics to think that they can be saved by lighting candles to Mary, or Baptists to think that they can be saved by going to church every Sunday and by carrying a Bible, or Lutherans to think they are saved if they have been baptized and confirmed.

If the personal spirit of religion is unsuccessful in preventing an individual from being saved, it then tries to keep that person from experiencing the fullness of salvation. It does not allow believers to move on to receive the filling of the Holy Spirit or freedom in Christ, or to enter into God's full destiny for their lives. Paul specifically warns that the devil, by his craftiness, can corrupt *minds* and keep them from "the simplicity that is in Christ" (2 Cor. 11:3).

The second Christendom-related office could be an Office of Corporate Church Structure. Here the spirit of religion targets the religious power brokers, who determine the destiny of whole organizations, such as denominations. The central issue is God's new times and seasons. The demonic strategy behind this is to preserve the status quo through adhering to what the Bible calls the tradition of the elders (see Matt. 15:2 and Mark 7:5).

THE CORPORATE SPIRIT OF RELIGION

That brings us to the subject of the rest of this chapter, namely what I think we might call the corporate spirit of religion. The authors of other chapters in this book will analyze and elaborate on many other manifestations of the spirit of religion. However, because in my personal area of ministry I deal constantly with hearing what the Spirit is saying to the churches collectively about new times and seasons, this corporate manifestation is the one I have been faced with the most. This is the only chapter in this book that specifically addresses the issue of the corporate spirit of religion.

Understanding the corporate spirit of religion is extremely important because we now live in the Second Apostolic Age (which I date as beginning in 2001) and we are currently witnessing the most radical change in the way of doing church since the Protestant Reformation. That is why I like to call what we are seeing the New Apostolic Reformation.[2]

So, how do we handle radical changes like this?

NEW WINESKINS

The most radical change recorded in the Bible was the change from the Old Covenant to the New Covenant. When Jesus addressed the disciples of John the Baptist, the last prominent representative of the Old Covenant, He used the terminology "old wineskin" and "new wineskin" (see Matt. 9:16-17). Jesus said that when God has new wine for His people, He pours it only into new wineskins. He doesn't pour it into old wineskins (which at one time, of course, were His new wineskins), because He loves them and He doesn't want to destroy them.

The change from an old wineskin to a new wineskin, such as the New Apostolic Reformation, always meets powerful resistance. However, the resistance does not come from the *anointed leaders* of the old wineskin. For instance, John the Baptist blessed the new wineskin, saying, "[Jesus] must increase, but I must decrease" (John 3:30). He said, "He who is coming after me is mightier than I" (Matt. 3:11). Nicodemus and Gamaliel would be other examples of anointed old-wineskin leaders.

No, the opposition to God's new changes always comes from the *unanointed leaders* of the old wineskin. For example, the attitude of the Pharisees was the opposite of John the Baptist's attitude. The Pharisees ended up killing Jesus! The last thing they were willing to do was to decrease and thereby lose the position of power that they were enjoying in the old wineskin.

What is going on? I see this as nothing less than the operation of a demonic force that I have been calling the corporate spirit of religion. It is a device of Satan. As I have already written, we must never allow ourselves to be ignorant of his devices. Therefore, let's try to understand this demonic spirit as well as possible.

THE ISSUE IS THE MIND

Daniel 2:21 tells us, "[God] changes the times and the seasons." Part of the character of God, then, is to continually produce new wine and to provide new wineskins for it. But Satan, of course, does not like that a bit, and later in the same book of Daniel, Satan reveals his purposes through the "fourth beast" who, according to the text, "shall persecute the saints of the Most

High, and shall intend to change times and law" (Dan. 7:25). What God designs for His glory and the advance of His kingdom, Satan constantly attacks in order to turn it back around.

What device does Satan use to attempt to roll back God's new times and seasons? Look at that phrase "persecute the saints." The Aramaic word for "persecute" is *belah*, which means to "wear out" the mind.[3] In other words, the corporate spirit of religion, as Satan's agent in this case, does not play so much on

Religious leaders can actually be living holy lives and still be under the influence of the spirit of religion.

the heart or on the emotions or on personal holiness or on the fruit of the Spirit, but rather on the *mind*. Religious leaders can actually be living holy lives and still be under the influence of the spirit of religion. It causes people, especially religious power brokers, to *think* the wrong thoughts.

This implies that the way we can best neutralize the power of the spirit of religion is to be "transformed by the renewing of [our] *mind*, that [we] may prove what is that good and acceptable and perfect will of God" (Rom. 12:2, emphasis added). A key to combating the religious spirit, then, is sound teaching, which helps people get their minds straight.

Paul, for example, strongly urged Timothy to be a good soldier and not to entangle himself with the affairs of this life. Notice his admonition to Timothy: "You therefore must endure hardship as a good soldier of Jesus Christ" (2 Tim. 2:3). Part of being a good soldier is getting your *mind* straight. This will combat the attacks of the spirit of religion.

FOUR CHARACTERISTICS OF THE CORPORATE SPIRIT OF RELIGION

If you have been an active believer for some time, chances are that you have come up against the corporate spirit of religion. Consequently, you may recognize these four characteristics.

1. *The corporate spirit of religion is a high-level demon.* It is probably on the level of some other principalities that are named in Scripture, such as Wormwood (see Rev. 8:11), Beelzebub (see Luke 11:15), the prince of Greece (see Dan. 10:20) and the queen of heaven (see Jer. 7:18).

2. *The corporate spirit of religion invades groups of people, not individuals.* Spirits that invade individuals, such as a spirit of rejection, a spirit of trauma, a spirit of lust or a personal religious spirit, all need to be cast out of its victims through deliverance ministry. Instead, the assignment of the corporate spirit of religion is collective. It casts a spell over the leaders of whole segments of God's people. This, for example, is reflected in Galatians 3:1: "O foolish Galatians! Who has bewitched you that you should not obey the truth . . . ?" That word "bewitched" is a very strong word. The Galatians as a whole church were under the spell of the corporate spirit of religion. They hesitated to move into God's new times and seasons for them. In this case the spell, which is a form of curse, needs to be renounced and broken through the blood of Jesus by the spiritual authorities

over the group. Then they can be transformed by the renewing of their minds, as it says in Romans 12:2. If they are not willing to do this, the spell will not leave, and individuals whose minds are renewed will be advised to leave the group.

3. *The corporate spirit of religion is extremely subtle.* This spirit doesn't speak out loud or write on walls or move furniture around the room. People under its influence have no clue to its existence. In fact, the corporate spirit of religion succeeds in making them *think* that they are actually doing God's will! For example, the Pharisees said to Jesus, in good faith: "Look, why do [your disciples, who were picking grain on the Sabbath] do what is not lawful?" (Mark 2:24). And "Why do Your disciples transgress the tradition of the elders? For they do not wash their hands when they eat bread" (Matt. 15:2). The Pharisees had elevated the tradition of the elders into a place equal to Scripture, believing that they were serving God by doing this.

4. *The corporate spirit of religion manipulates leaders into opposing God's plan for new times and seasons.* A good case in point is Peter. When he was with Jesus in Caesarea Philippi, he had one of his best days one morning and one of his worst days the same afternoon. He started off by declaring that Jesus was "the Christ, the Son of the living God" (Matt. 16:16). Jesus' encouraging response was, "Blessed are you, Simon Bar-Jonah, for flesh and blood has not revealed this to you, but My Father who is in heaven" (v. 17). That was a really good day for Peter.

But not for long. Later that same day Jesus told

His disciples that He was going to leave them. In other words, times and seasons would change for the disciples. Peter didn't like that. He preferred the status quo and he told Jesus so in no uncertain terms. Look at Jesus' response: "Get behind Me, Satan!" (v. 23). Peter had done a 180 within a matter of hours, and Jesus traced Peter's statement to the realm of darkness. Jesus continued, "You are an offense to Me, for you are not mindful of the things of God, but the things of men" (v. 23). I don't think it would be stretching things too far to suppose that Satan's agent for making Peter, who was spokesperson for the group, think the wrong way that afternoon would be the corporate spirit of religion.

THE MODUS OPERANDI

Jesus tells us seven times in the book of Revelation that we need to hear what the Spirit is saying to the churches. The tense of the verb "say" is present tense, not past tense, which means that the Holy Spirit is still speaking. What the Holy Spirit said to the churches then is vitally important for us to hear today. Much of it is found on the inspired pages of Scripture, but the Spirit did not stop speaking when the canon of the Bible was concluded. The Holy Spirit continually speaks new things that we should not only hear, but also obey.

However, the corporate spirit of religion does not want us to hear these new things from God. How does this demon keep us from it? Belah! It tries to wear us out mentally, so much that we cannot hear. We become spiritually insensitive. When the Holy Spirit speaks to us about a new wineskin, the corporate spirit of religion springs into action among the leaders of the old wineskin. It manipulates the minds of religious power brokers to emphasize what the Spirit *said* (past tense) to them back in the days when they were leaders of a new wineskin.

Let's take for example the Holy Spirit's move of recognizing the contemporary offices of prophet and apostle. Some old-wineskin leaders might reject the idea of apostolic authority and leadership because they already are committed to church structures that emphasize democratic power sharing and decision making. They might conclude that since democracy worked in the past, it will always work. This prevents them from moving into God's new times and seasons. I have seen things like this happen time and time again.

In order to accomplish its purposes, the corporate spirit of religion administers what could be described as an intravenous injection of *fear*. Old-wineskin leaders fear losing their positions of power. They fear being pulled out of their comfort zones. Their typical question is, "What am I going to *lose* by moving into God's new times and seasons?" They rarely ask, instead, "What is the kingdom of God going to *gain*?" They are hesitant to risk the possibility of either losing control or losing money. So they capitulate to the religious spirit and do whatever it takes to preserve the status quo, while honestly thinking that they are doing God's will.

THE LINK WITH THE SPIRIT OF POLITICS

It is worthy of mention that the ultimate tactic of the corporate spirit of religion is to form an alliance with the spirit of politics. This is how the Pharisees ended up killing Jesus.

The Pharisees were out to do away with Jesus. He was the most serious threat to their religious status quo that they had encountered. "[Jesus] entered the synagogue again, and a man was there who had a withered hand. And [the Pharisees] watched

Him closely, whether He would heal him on the Sabbath, so that they might accuse Him" (Mark 3:1-2).

However, the Pharisees knew that, under Roman law, they would have no power to eliminate Jesus. So they sought out political means. "The Pharisees went out and immediately plotted with the Herodians against [Jesus], how they might destroy Him" (Mark 3:6). The Herodians were a Jewish group that had the favor of the dynasty of Herod. They were not traditional allies of the Pharisees, but when the Pharisees allied with them, linking the spirit of religion with the spirit of politics, it was only a matter of time until Jesus would be crucified.

I mention this because this alliance is common in the world today. For example, the spirit of religion in the Roman Catholic Church for centuries linked with the political spirit in Latin America and effectively prevented the spread of the gospel. Once this was broken, evangelical churches began to mushroom. Currently, some Eastern European countries that have come out of Communist atheism are in danger of curtailing their new religious freedom by making an alliance with Orthodox churches, which are seeking to prevent the spread of non-Orthodox churches in their midst. The Orthodox Church wants governments to recognize it as the only official Christian Church and to enact antimissionary laws. Likewise, anticonversion laws in Hindu lands represent this deadly linking of the religious spirit with the political spirit.

THREE PRINCIPLES FOR DEALING WITH THE SPIRIT OF RELIGION

How do those of us who feel that God has assigned us to move into new wineskins deal with the opposition of the spirit of religion? I clearly recall the battle I had when, with John Wimber, I tried to introduce signs and wonders into the curriculum of

Fuller Seminary back in the 1980s. The power brokers of the seminary did not want this new wineskin in their midst. The spirit of religion was strong enough to convince them that they were actually serving God by not allowing healing or deliverance in their seminary classrooms.

Looking back to those years, which, by the way, constituted the most painful period of my entire ministry, I can draw some principles for dealing with the spirit of religion. The upshot of my implementing these principles was that healing and deliverance ultimately became part of the school's curriculum, so these principles may have some validity.

1. *Don't get sidetracked.* The corporate spirit of religion would love to weaken you by consuming your time and energy. It frequently uses enticements such as "Let's dialogue" or "We need more prayer" or "Do further study" or "Give the old wineskin another chance." All of this is designed to wear out your mind, the literal meaning of "belah." In the signs and wonders controversy at Fuller Seminary, I was forced into a good bit of this against my will, and I was weakened by it.

2. *Engage in warfare.* Keep in mind that the battle is a spiritual battle, because behind it all, evil spirits are trying to disrupt God's plans. The Bible says, "The weapons of our warfare are not carnal but mighty in God" for doing several things, including "bringing every *thought* into captivity to the obedience of Christ" (2 Cor. 10:4-5, emphasis added). We use our spiritual authority through the blood of Christ to bind the corporate spirit of religion, which is trying to make leaders think wrong thoughts.

I attribute the resolution of our conflicts at Fuller Seminary, more than anything else, to the aggressive, prophetic intercession of my prayer partners. If space permitted, I could give specific instances of how their warfare prayer actually changed the minds of some of those who had been determined to bring me down. However, because it was real warfare, I am sorry to report that others saw their careers at the seminary come to a premature end.

3. *Show your opponents honor and respect.* Keep in mind that the people who come against you are not your enemies. Your real enemy, the corporate spirit of religion, is simply using certain individuals to accomplish its ungodly desires to maintain the status quo. This is the time to clothe ourselves with humility, as 1 Peter 5:5 tells us to do, because "God resists the proud, but gives grace to the humble."

At Fuller Seminary there was a coalition of five faculty members who decided to take me on. I was able to avoid one-on-one polemics with all five. I don't recall ever tearing them down behind their backs. Why? They were good people. I had no question that each one of them deeply desired to serve God. They were upset with me only because they, unknowingly, had come under the influence of a religious spirit.

The spirit of religion is defeated when its victims become transformed by the renewing of their minds, according to Romans 12:2. This will happen to those who, like John the Baptist, become anointed leaders of the old wineskin; and together we will be ready to move triumphantly into our new times, our new seasons and our new destinies.

Chapter Two

THE CORPORATE SPIRIT OF RELIGION IN ACTION—A CASE STUDY

JIM ANDERSON

Jim Anderson lives in Blaine, Minnesota, a suburb of St. Paul and Minneapolis. He has been married to Dawn for 30-plus happy years. Their lives have been enriched with three sons and a daughter.

Jim serves as the lead pastor of the Harbor Church in Cottage Grove/Hastings, Minnesota. He is also the president of Harvest Impact Consulting, which coaches established churches in their quest to be healthy, outreach-oriented communities.

In June 2005, Jim became the presiding overseer of Harvest Network International (HNI), which he helped found in 1985. Today, HNI is an international network linking over 40 apostolic movements in 23 nations. It seeks to be a unifying force for Great Commission work by joining churches and ministries in North America with international leaders in church planting, leadership development and meaningful service in the name of Jesus Christ.

It was in December 2003 that I first heard C. Peter Wagner offer Daniel 7:25 as a clear statement of the primary goals of the corporate spirit of religion. This verse, which speaks of the fourth beast (the manifestation of evil in Daniel's vision) reads, "He will speak against the Most High and oppress his saints and try to change the set times and the laws. The saints will be handed over to him for a time, times and half a time" (*NIV*). Five strategies of the enemy are summarized in this verse:

- To slander God's character and intent ("He will speak against the Most High")
- To oppress God's people through fear and discouragement ("and oppress [God's] saints")
- To delay the emergence of the new times and seasons that God has set for His Kingdom's advancement ("and try to change the set times")
- To promote the creeping rise of liberalism, or disloyalty to God's laws and ways ("and the laws")
- To persecute the saints outrightly ("The saints will be handed over to him for a time, times and half a time")

Leaders who make ongoing renewal of Christ's Church one of their primary objectives will have to deal with all of these strategies of the enemy at some point. Many new Christians anticipate that most of the opposition they will endure will come from the demonic realm and from people who are not a part of Christ's Church. However, one quickly learns that this is not always true. We soon realize that strong opposition to change often comes from within the Body of Christ. This opposition comes from well-meaning traditionalists and what many of us have come to call the spirit of religion, or more specifically the corporate spirit of religion.

This evil principality works within the Church to fan into flame a natural human passion to preserve the "tradition of the elders," as the Pharisees expressed it in Mark 7:5. Peter Wagner has accurately characterized this mind-set brought about by the corporate spirit of religion as one that allows what God said in the past to keep us from hearing what God is saying today. In Mark 7:9, Jesus told us to beware of prejudice in favor of the familiar. He warned that our hearts can easily set aside a passionate obedience to God's present commands (both scriptural and prophetic) because we have fallen into an adulterous affair of the heart with our traditions.

A Personal Encounter with the Corporate Spirit of Religion

In the mid-1980s I learned that opposition to change in the Church does not only come from non-Christians and traditional denominational structures. If we are not careful, it can gain a firm foothold even among renewal ministries and reformers. Within the course of one or two decades, the very structures that we establish to transform the church can fall prey to spiritual forces and human impulses that resist God's ongoing plans. It doesn't take long!

From the early 1970s through the late 1980s, I was privileged to be a part of the charismatic movement among traditional Lutherans in the United States. As the Lord poured out His Spirit across the nation during that season, many renewal committees developed in states or larger regions. Most of the other major denominations also had a national charismatic committee of some kind. The national renewal ministry among charismatic Lutherans was based in the upper Midwest. This ministry held an annual convention that, at its height in the mid-1970s, drew nearly 20,000 attendees from North America and other nations.

The foundational strategic assumption of the charismatic renewal movement in the United States throughout the 1970s was

> **If we are not careful, opposition to change in the Church can gain a firm foothold even among renewal ministries and reformers.**

that God intended to renew the mainline institutional denominations through the persistent witness of its charismatic members on the inside. However, by the early 1980s, two realities seemed to be challenging this assumption. First, there was a definite lack of results. By 1980, an estimated 15 percent of all Lutheran lay people and clergy had experienced some kind of spiritual renewal through the charismatic renewal. Though most of these tens of thousands of people remained in their Lutheran churches and prayed for renewal of the old wineskins, only three dozen churches had become what could be termed renewal churches.

Second, there loomed ahead plans for a massive merger that was designed to unite three major Lutheran bodies into what is today the Evangelical Lutheran Church in America (ELCA). Many charismatic Lutherans in these three uniting groups suggested that the ELCA's proposed constitution was weak in defining the place of Scripture. There was considerable concern among them that the new denomination would drift toward unbiblical positions on issues like same-sex unions and the ordination of homosexuals.

THE FIRST ENCOUNTER

As director of a small regional Lutheran renewal ministry in the northeastern United States, I was one of the younger leaders involved in the top levels of national leadership. At the time, I was 15- to 20-years younger than the generation of clergy and lay leaders who pioneered this awakening among Lutherans. I considered it a great privilege to serve alongside leaders whom I considered to be my mentors. Living in upstate New York, I flew to the national headquarters several times a year to attend meetings of the national renewal committee's oversight board.

Around the early 1980s, prophetic voices within the ranks of the Lutheran renewal movement began to indicate that a significant strategic change was about to take place. These proven prophetic leaders began to speak of disengaging from efforts to renew the old wineskin of Lutheran denominational structures. The prophets indicated that a new season of outreach and evangelism was at hand. They called for an end to the failed monolithic strategy of Lutheran renewal, and they spoke of the birth of new subgroups with more focused objectives. This, quite assuredly, was a major change in perspective.

It was in the spring of 1986 that I first witnessed the influence of the spirit of religion seeking to resist the new God-directed times and seasons of the national Lutheran renewal movement. At a meeting of the national board, an article that raised the possibilities of new strategies was discussed at length. The prophetic were brought to the table for consideration. A proposal was made to host a strategic summit for all Lutheran charismatic leaders in North America to consider new strategies and seek God's guidance concerning the coming ELCA merger.

At that point, the national board's chairman, whom I shall call Karl (not his real name), stunned me by recommending that no response at all be made to either the merger plans or the prophetic words. His rationale for this non-response was twofold. First, he felt it would confuse the Lutheran charismatic laypeople, who for 15 years had been told to remain in their Lutheran congregations and to bloom where they were planted, as the saying goes. He asserted that it would be better to remain consistent, despite the lack of fruit seen over the previous 15 years. Second, he argued that new strategies that might encourage some Lutherans to leave their congregations could offend traditional institutional church leaders.

After a heated discussion, I was amazed to watch as all but two of the board members backed Karl's recommendation that no response be made to the prophetic words. A vote on hosting a leaders' summit to consider the implications of the ELCA merger was rejected almost unanimously. I walked away from that meeting feeling confused and disillusioned. I could not understand how a group of seasoned national leaders, who knew how to move with the Holy Spirit, would fail to gather and give leadership to their renewal-oriented constituents at such a historic moment.

AN AMAZING REVERSAL

A few days after that meeting, the Lord told me to host a national leaders' summit for Lutheran charismatics in my hometown in upstate New York. After some serious prayer, I accepted this challenge and began praying about whom to invite as main speakers. To my great consternation I felt strongly led by the Spirit to invite most of the leaders from the national renewal committee, who only weeks before had voted against meeting to consider the ELCA merger.

I made the calls, and I was amazed as each leader whom I invited to speak accepted immediately. Most of them added comments to the effect that they believed this leaders' summit was desperately needed at this time. Of course, I asked them why they had changed their minds. It seemed that each one, upon leaving the spiritual atmosphere of the national board meeting, had found his outlook completely changed.

Why, without talking among themselves, would a dozen decisive leaders change their minds so completely? I believe the corporate spirit of religion had been able to create a fear of departing from the strategies of the past. Somehow Karl had submitted to the influence of this spirit, and his leadership of the national board had spread the spirit's influence. This corporate spirit of religion had controlled these strong leaders by stirring in them an irrational loyalty to their denomination, which in turn had successfully blocked their ability to act on real data or on tested prophetic direction.

Once I acted upon these prophetic words and decided to convene the new summit, it seemed that the power of the spirit of religion had been broken. The national summit was held in September 1987 with most of the national board leaders fully involved. That event turned out to be a milestone. It changed the strategy of the Lutheran charismatic movement in the United States, setting thousands of Spirit-filled Lutherans free to follow their Lord's guidance into more fruitful involvement in the great harvest. It also helped birth three new submovements and it strengthened several preexisting conservative Lutheran groups.

THE SECOND ENCOUNTER

Nevertheless, an ideological struggle between the new, multi-strategy tactics and the traditional approach to Lutheran renewal continued over the next several years. I became identified as a key proponent of the new wineskin of Lutheran renewal, since I had served as the host of the 1987 National Lutheran Charismatic Leaders' Summit, where the shift had occurred. In May of 1988, I was invited to speak at the annual conference of charismatic Lutherans in Florida and Georgia. By the time of that conference, I represented one of several new apostolic associations that had formed following the ELCA merger. Karl, still the leader of the traditional national Lutheran renewal body, was asked to present the case for remaining in the ELCA.

As I was flying in to Orlando for that meeting, the Holy Spirit suddenly spoke to me three distinct words: "intimidation," "manipulation" and "control." I asked Him for further understanding, but received none at that time. I wrote them down, but did not think of them any further.

Upon arriving at the conference hotel, I came across Karl in the lobby. He greeted me warmly and invited me to have dinner with him that evening in the hotel restaurant. I was happy to do so.

As our dinner began, I was surprised to hear Karl tell me that he saw me as one of the most significant young leaders in Lutheran renewal. He invited me to write regularly for his national Lutheran renewal newsletter. He spoke of providing funding from the national ministry's budget in order to further my regional work and he asked me to consider merging my regional ministry with the national office. Karl went on to imply that he saw me, in the future, playing a major role in leading the national renewal.

As the conversation went on, I felt myself being drawn—almost trancelike—into Karl's flattery and praise. Suddenly, like a slap in the face, it occurred to me that his proposals were completely unworkable, from my point of view. I sensed that his ideas would neutralize what God had called me to do, so I asked him how we could possibly partner together, since our visions for renewal among Lutherans were headed in opposite directions. I respectfully thanked him for his offers—but firmly declined them.

When Karl heard my reply, his tone and demeanor changed dramatically. His face became distorted with anger, and he began to threaten me. He vowed that he would print things in his newsletter to destroy me. This sudden change of demeanor was frightening. I hardly knew what to do. I remember that I actually leaned back in my chair to try to put distance between us.

At that moment the Holy Spirit brought back to my mind the three words He had spoken to me on the plane that morning. I realized that He had given me those words as weapons to resist the evil spirit that was confronting me. I also realized that it was not Karl who was speaking, but a wicked spirit that was speaking through him. When I realized this, a great peace came over me. Using the three words God had given me that morning, I simply said, "Karl, I feel like you are trying to intimidate, manipulate and control me." Karl was immediately transformed. His anger vanished and he went back to eating and conversing calmly as if nothing had happened. He did not, it seemed, remember anything that had just transpired at that table. I believe true deliverance had occurred.

Karl and I have never again discussed that evening's events. The next day at the conference we carried on a cordial debate, and we have sustained a distant, but respectful friendship ever since. The national Lutheran renewal movement still exists today, but it is now under new leadership and involved in pioneering a new apostolic reformation movement among people of Lutheran heritage.

THE LESSONS I LEARNED

Looking back on these events, I have come to believe that I witnessed a manifestation of the corporate spirit of religion. I took away three valuable lessons from the experience that have significantly shaped my leadership philosophy.

First, Satan does not wait long to attack any work of God, even relatively new movements. He will always be at work attempting to change the set times of God's emerging agenda by any means possible. I am now aware that God will regularly require of me bold, new steps of obedience. These new steps always involve organizational and personal risk. "Keeping up with Jesus" is not easy work. Only those willing to learn, change and risk will know the joy of high-impact leadership for a lifetime.

Second, I have learned to never underestimate the seductive power of the corporate spirit of religion. I am convinced that the petition "Lead us not into temptation, but deliver us from the evil one ["evil," KJV]" in the Lord's Prayer is a vital daily expression of our dependence on God's protection from the seductive, discouraging, delaying and liberalizing influence of this spirit, as well as protection from other attacks. I look back at God's faithfulness to me in revealing the spirit's strategy of intimidation, manipulation and control as a practical manifestation of God's love and care. I am grateful and dependent on the Father's daily love and protection.

Finally, I have learned that resisting the corporate spirit of religion will often force us to walk paths far different from the paths chosen by longtime companions and friends. Of course, we must always place following God's agenda for our lives ahead of human friendships—the forward movement of the Kingdom depends upon such obedience. But separation need not lead to shattered relationships. It can be our privilege to remain connected to the lives and ministries of longtime friends if we learn to walk in a gentle balance of grace and truth. This gives our Lord joy and brings Him much glory!

Chapter Three

COMBATING THE SPIRIT OF RELIGION

RICK JOYNER

Rick Joyner is the founder, executive director and senior pastor of MorningStar Fellowship Church. Rick is a well-known author of more than 30 books, including his latest, The Torch and the Sword, *which is his long-awaited sequel to* The Final Quest *and* The Call. *He also oversees the MorningStar School of Ministry, Fellowship of Ministries and Fellowship of Churches. Rick and his wife, Julie, live in North Carolina with their five children, Anna, Aaryn, Amber, Ben and Sam.*

Loving God is the greatest commandment and the greatest gift that we can possess. The second greatest commandment is to love our neighbors. As the Lord affirmed, the whole Law is fulfilled by keeping these two commandments. That is, if we keep these two commandments, we will keep the whole Law (see Matt. 22:34-40; Rom. 13:8).

Simple love for God will overcome most of the evil in our hearts, and it is the most powerful weapon against evil in the world. Because loving God is our highest goal, it must be the primary focus of our lives. This is why one of the enemy's most deceptive and deadly attacks upon the Church is meant to divert us from this ultimate quest. It is his strategy to keep us focused on the evil in our lives, knowing that we will become what we are beholding (see 2 Cor. 3:18). As long as we keep looking at the evil, it will continue to have dominion over us.

This is not to imply that we should ignore the sins and errors that are in our lives. In fact, the Scriptures command us to examine and test ourselves to be sure that we are still in the faith (see 2 Cor. 13:5). The issue is what we do after the iniquity is discovered. Do we turn to the tree of life? Do we try to make ourselves better so that we will then be acceptable to God, or do we turn to the cross of Jesus to find both the forgiveness and the power to overcome the sin?

A primary strategy of the enemy is intended to keep us focused on the evil, partaking of the tree of the knowledge of good and evil, instead of on the glory of the Lord and the cross. This is a tactic of the religious spirit, an evil spirit that is the counterfeit of the true love of God and of true worship. I wouldn't be surprised if this religious spirit has done more damage to the Church than have done the New Age movement and all the other cults combined.

THE NATURE OF THE SPIRIT OF RELIGION

The spirit of religion is a demon that seeks to substitute religious activity for the power of the Holy Spirit in our lives. Its primary objective is to have the Church "holding to a form of godliness, although they have denied its power" (2 Tim. 3:5, *NASB*). The apostle Paul completed his exhortation with *"avoid* such men as these" (v. 5, *NASB*, emphasis added). This religious spirit is the "leaven of the Pharisees and the Sadducees" (Matt. 16:6), of which the Lord warned us to beware.

The Lord often used metaphors to illustrate the lessons He taught because their characteristics were similar. The religious spirit does operate like the leaven in bread. It does not add substance or nutritional value to the bread—it only inflates it. Such is the by-product of the religious spirit. It does not add to the life and power of the Church, but merely feeds the very pride of man that caused the Fall, and almost every fall since.

Satan seems to understand even better than the Church that "God resists the proud, but gives grace to the humble" (Jas. 4:6). He knows very well that God will not inhabit any work that is inflated with pride and that God Himself will even resist such a work. So Satan's strategy is to make us proud—even proud of good things, such as how much we read the Bible, witness or feed the poor. He knows that if we do the will of God in pride, our work will be counterproductive and could ultimately work toward our fall.

Satan also knows that once leaven gets into the bread, it is extremely difficult to remove. Pride, by its very nature, is the most difficult stronghold to remove or correct. The religious spirit keeps us from hearing the voice of God by encouraging us to assume that we already know God's opinion, what He is saying and what pleases Him. This delusion is the result of believing that God is just like us. It could even cause us to rationalize our need to obey Scripture, having us believe that rebukes, exhortations and words of correction are for other people, but not for us.

If the religious spirit is a problem in your life, you have probably already begun to think about how badly someone you know needs to read this message. It may not even have occurred to you that God put this into your hands because *you* need it. In fact, we all need to keep our guard up, because the religious spirit is one enemy that all of us are very susceptible to. It is imperative that we remain free of its devastating deception.

THE GREAT DECEPTION

One of the most deceptive characteristics about the religious spirit is that it is founded upon zeal for God. We tend to think that zeal for God could never be evil, however that depends on *why* we are zealous for Him.

Paul wrote of his Jewish brethren in Romans 10:2, "For I bear them witness that they have a *zeal* for God, but not according to knowledge" (emphasis added). At that time of Paul, no one on the earth prayed more, fasted more, read the Bible more, had a greater hope in the coming of the Messiah or had more zeal for the things of God than did the Pharisees. Yet these religious leaders turned out to be the greatest opposers of God and His Messiah when Christ came.

Those who are truly zealous are the most difficult to deal with, so the enemy's strategy against them is to push their zeal too far. His first step is to get them to glory in their own zeal. Regardless of how important a gift we might have, if the enemy can get us to take pride in it, he will have us in his snare and will begin to use that gift for evil.

The Lord had little trouble with most demons while He walked the earth. They quickly recognized His authority and they begged for mercy. But the religious spirit was different. It was embedded in the conservative, zealous religious leaders, who immediately became Jesus' greatest enemies. Those who were the most zealous for the Word of God ended up crucifying the Word Himself when He became flesh to walk among them. The same is still true.

> **All of the cults and false religions combined have not done as much damage to the moves of God as the infiltration of the spirit of religion into the Church.**

As I have said, all of the cults and false religions combined have not done as much damage to the moves of God as the infiltration of the spirit of religion into the Church. Cults and false religions are easily discerned and discarded, but the religious spirit is extremely subtle. It has attempted to thwart possibly every revival or movement of God to date, and it still retains an undeserved seat of honor throughout a huge part of today's Church.

THE FOUNDATION OF PRIDE

Idealism is one of the most deceptive and destructive disguises of the religious spirit. Idealism is of human origin and is a form of humanism. Although it has the appearance of seeking only the highest standards and the preservation of God's glory, idealism is possibly the most deadly enemy of true revelation and true grace. It is deadly because it does not allow for growing up into grace and wisdom; rather it attacks and destroys the foundation of those who are in pursuit of God's glory but who have not arrived yet.

Idealism makes us try to impose on others standards that are beyond that which God has required or has given the grace for at that time. For example, those who are controlled by this kind of religious spirit may condemn others who may not pray two hours a day as they do. The truth is that God's will for others might not be the same as for us. The grace of God may call us to pray, in a certain season, say 10 minutes a day. Then as we become so blessed by His presence, we will want to spend more and more time with Him until we will not want to quit after just 10 minutes. If we are eventually praying two hours a day, it will be because of our love for prayer and the presence of the Lord, not out of fear or pride caused by the spirit of religion.

When the religious spirit succeeds in producing pride, it leads to *perfectionism*. The perfectionist person sees everything as black or white. This develops extremes, requiring that every person and every teaching be judged as either 100 percent right or 100 percent wrong. This is a standard of perfection that only Jesus could comply with. It will lead to a serious delusion when we impose it on ourselves or on others. True grace imparts a truth that sets people free, showing them the way out of their sin and beckoning them to higher levels of spiritual maturity.

Those who have the religious spirit may be able to point out problems with great accuracy, but they seldom have solutions, except to tear down what has already been built. The strategy of the enemy is to nullify progress that is being made and to sow discouragement that will limit future progress.

The perfectionist both imposes and tries to live by standards that actually stifle true maturity and growth. The grace of God will lead us up the mountain step-by-step. The Lord does not condemn us because we may trip a few times while trying to climb. He graciously picks us up with the encouragement that we can make it. We must have a vision of making it to the top, and we should never condemn ourselves for not being there yet *as long as we are still climbing.*

THE DEADLY COMBINATION

One of the most powerful and deceptive forms of the religious spirit is built upon a combination of fear and pride. Those who are bound in this way go through periods of deep anguish and remorse at their failures, but this false repentance results only in more self-abasement and further attempts to make sacrifices that will appease the Lord. Then they often flip to the other side, becoming so convinced that they are superior to other Christians or other groups that they become unteachable and unable to receive reproof. The foundation that they stand on at any given time will be dictated more by external pressure than by true conviction.

Such a religious spirit is so slippery that it will wiggle out of almost any attempt to confront it. If you address the pride, the fears and insecurities will rise up to attract sympathy. If you confront the fear, it will then change into religious pride masquerading as faith. This type of spirit will drive individuals or congregations to such extremes that they will inevitably disintegrate.

THE COUNTERFEIT GIFT OF DISCERNMENT

The religious spirit will often produce a counterfeit gift of discernment of spirits. This counterfeit gift thrives on seeing what is wrong with others rather than on seeing what God is doing in people so that we can help them along. This is how the religious spirit does some of its greatest damage to the Church. Its evil work will almost always leave more damage and division than it does healing and reconciliation. Its mind-set is rooted in the tree of the knowledge of good and evil, and though some of the truth it proclaims may be accurate, it is ministered in a spirit that kills.

This counterfeit gift of discernment is motivated by suspicion and fear. The suspicion is rooted in such things as rejection, territorial preservation or general insecurity. However, the true gift of discernment can only function through love. Any motive other than love will destroy spiritual perception. Whenever someone submits a judgment or criticism about another person or group, we should disregard it unless we know that the one bringing it truly loves that person or group.

THE TEST OF A TRUE MESSENGER

In Ezekiel 37 the Lord took the prophet Ezekiel to a valley full of dry bones and asked him whether the bones could live. The Lord then commanded him, "Prophesy to these bones" (v. 4). As Ezekiel prophesied, the bones came together and came to life, and then became a great army (see vv. 7-10).

This is an important test through which every true ministry must pass. The true prophet can see a great army in even the driest of bones. He will prophesy life to those bones until they come to life and become an army. A false prophet with the religious spirit will do little more then just tell the bones how dry they are, heaping discouragement and condemnation on them, but imparting no life or power to overcome their circumstances.

Apostles and prophets are given authority to build up and tear down, but they have no right to tear down if they have not first built up. We should give no one the authority to bring correction to the people under our care unless they first have a history of providing spiritual nourishment and building people up. Some people may say that such a policy would eliminate the ministry of the prophets altogether, but I say that so-called prophets who do not have a heart to build others up should be eliminated from ministry. As Jude said of them, these people are "hidden reefs in your love feasts" (Jude 12, *NASB*). They are "grumblers, finding fault" (v. 16, *NASB*). They have come under the power of the spirit of religion.

THE ROOT OF SELF-RIGHTEOUSNESS

The religious spirit will make us feel very good about our spiritual condition as long as we are self-centered and self-seeking. Pride feels good; it can even be exhilarating. But it keeps all of our attention on how well we are doing and on how we stand compared to others—not on how we stand compared to the glory of God. This results in our putting confidence in discipline and personal sacrifice rather than in the Lord and His sacrifice.

Of course, discipline and a commitment to self-sacrifice are essential qualities for every believer to have. But it is the *motivation* behind them that determines whether we are being driven by the religious spirit or being led by the Holy Spirit. The religious spirit motivates through fear and guilt, or through pride and ambition. The motivation of the Holy Spirit is love for the Son of God.

Delighting in self-abasement is a sure symptom of the religious spirit. This does not mean that we should neglect to fast or to discipline our bodies, as Paul did (see 1 Cor. 9:27). However, the problem comes when we take a perverse delight in this, rather than taking delight in the Son of God.

DECEPTIVE REVELATION

Colossians 2:18-19 indicates that those with the religious spirit will tend to delight in self-abasement and will often be given to worshiping angels or taking improper stands on visions they have seen. The religious spirit wants us to worship anything or anyone except Jesus. The same spirit that influences us to worship angels will also push us to excessively exalt people.

Consequently, we must beware of anyone who unduly exalts angels or men and women of God, or anyone who uses the visions that he or she has received to gain improper influence in the Church. God does not give us revelations so that people will respect us more or to exalt our ministries. The fruit of true revelation will be humility, not pride.

THE MARTYR SYNDROME

When combined with the religious spirit, the martyr syndrome is one of the ultimate and most deadly delusions. To be a true martyr for the faith, literally losing our lives for the sake of Christ, is one of the greatest honors that we could receive. Yet when this is perverted, it becomes a most tragic form of deception.

When the religious spirit succeeds in producing a martyr syndrome, it is almost impossible for that person to be delivered from the deception that he or she is "suffering for the gospel." At this point, any rejection or correction received from others is perceived as the price to be paid in order to "stand for the truth." This warped perspective will drive them even further from the truth and any possibility of correction.

The martyr syndrome can also be a manifestation of the spirit of suicide. For some people, it seems easier to "die for the Lord" than to live for Him. Those who have a perverted understanding of the Cross glory more in death than they do in life. They fail to see that the point of the Cross is resurrection, not the grave.

THE EARLY WARNING SIGNS OF THE SPIRIT OF RELIGION

Our goal must be to get completely free of any influence from the religious spirit by being completely submitted to the Holy Spirit. Without this submission to the Lord, there is no way to be delivered from the religious spirit.

Through many years of ministry I have observed the spirit of religion closely. It has attacked me on more than one occasion. I have watched its devastating effects in the lives of other believers. In many cases I have helped people to recognize the pernicious inroads of this spirit into their lives, and I have helped them to be delivered and to enter into the true freedom of life in Christ.

As I have confronted this spirit, I have developed a checklist of 25 early warning signs that frequently appear. I would encourage you to prayerfully go through this list. First ask God to show you to what degree any of these traits apply to your own life. This may not be easy, because the spirit of religion is so subtle and deceptive. If you find one or more of these things in your life, boldly rebuke that filthy spirit and command it to leave in the name of Jesus. Be free and be clean.

It is only after you do that that you can begin to use the list to detect the religious spirit in others in order to help them. However, if you try this without being an overcomer yourself, you are probably showing a symptom that you have a serious problem. Take heed of Paul's instruction: "Test yourselves to see if you are in the faith" (2 Cor. 13:5, *NASB*).

1. *People with the religious spirit will often see their primary mission as the tearing down of whatever they believe is wrong.* Such a person's ministry will result more in division than in lasting works that are bearing fruit for the Kingdom.

2. *They will be unable to accept a rebuke, especially from those whom they judge to be less spiritual than they.* Think back on how *you* responded the last few times someone tried to correct you.

3. *They will have a philosophy that says, "I will not listen to people, but only to God."* Since God frequently speaks through people, this is an obvious delusion, revealing serious spiritual pride.

4. *They will be inclined to see more of what is wrong with other people, other churches and so on, than what is right with them.* From the valley John saw Babylon, but when he was carried to a high mountain, he saw the new Jerusalem (see Rev. 21:10). If we are only seeing Babylon, it is because of our perspective. Those who are in a place of true vision will have their attention on what God is doing, not on what people are doing.

5. *They will be subject to an overwhelming feeling of guilt that they can never measure up to the Lord's standards.* This is a root of the religious spirit, because it causes us to base our relationship with Him on our performance rather than on the Cross. Jesus has already measured up for us. He is the completed work that the Father is seeking to accomplish within us. Our whole goal in life should be simply to abide in Him.

6. *They will keep score on their spiritual life.* This includes feeling better about ourselves because we do what we consider to be spiritual, such as go to more meetings,

read the Bible more and do more things for the Lord. These are all noble endeavors, but the true measure of spiritual maturity is getting closer to God.

7. *They will believe that they have been appointed to fix everyone else.* These persons become the self-appointed watchmen, or sheriffs, in God's kingdom. They are seldom involved in building, but serve only to keep the Church in a state of annoyance and agitation, if not causing serious divisions.

8. *They will have a leadership style that is bossy, overbearing and intolerant of the weaknesses or failures of others.* However, as James wrote, "the wisdom from above is first pure, then peaceable, gentle, reasonable, full of mercy and good fruits, unwavering, without hypocrisy. And the seed whose fruit is righteousness is sown in peace by those who make peace" (Jas. 3:17-18, *NASB*).

9. *They will have a sense that they are closer to God than other people are or that their lives or ministries are more pleasing to Him.* This is a symptom of the profound delusion that we draw closer to God because of who we are, rather than through Jesus.

10. *People with the religious spirit will take pride in their spiritual maturity and discipline, especially as compared with others.* True spiritual maturity involves growing up into Christ. When we begin to compare ourselves with others, it is obvious that we have lost sight of the true goal—Jesus.

11. *They will believe that they are on the cutting edge of what God is doing.* This includes thinking that we are involved in the most important thing that God is doing.

12. *They will have a mechanical prayer life.* When we start feeling relief when our prayer time is over or when we have prayed through our prayer list, we should consider our condition. We should never feel relief when our conversations with the One we love are over.

13. *They will do things in order to be noticed by people.* This is a symptom of the idolatry of fearing people more than we fear God, which results in a religion that serves people instead of God.

14. *They will be overly repulsed by emotionalism.* When people who are subject to the religious spirit encounter the true life of God, it will usually appear to them to be excessive, emotional and carnal. True passion for God is often emotional and demonstrative, such as David exemplified when he brought the Ark of God into Jerusalem (see 2 Sam. 6:14-16).

15. *They will use emotionalism as a substitute for the work of the Holy Spirit.* This seems contradictory to the previous point, but the religious spirit will often take contradictory positions in its drive for self-preservation and exaltation. This use of emotionalism will include such things as requiring weeping and wailing as evidence of repentance, or "falling under the power" as evidence that one has been touched by God. Both of these can be evidences of the true work of the Holy Spirit. It is when we require these manifestations that we are beginning to move in another spirit.

    During the First Great Awakening, for example, Jonathan Edwards' meetings would often have some of the toughest, most rebellious men falling to the ground and staying there for up to 24 hours. They would get up changed. Such strange manifestations of the Holy Spirit fueled the Great Awakening. Even so, Edwards stated that people who faked the manifestations did more to bring an end to the Great Awakening than did the enemies of the revival!

16. *They will be encouraged when their ministries look better than others.* We could include in this being discouraged when it seems that others are looking better or growing faster than we are.

17. *They will glory more in what God did in the past than in what He is doing in the present.* God has not changed— He is the same yesterday, today and forever. The veil has been removed, and we can be as close to God today as anyone ever has been in the past. The religious spirit will always seek to focus our attention on doing good work and on making comparisons, rather than on simply drawing closer to the Lord.

18. *They will tend to be suspicious of or oppose new movements, new churches and other new things that God brings to life.* This is an obvious symptom of jealousy, a primary fruit of the religious spirit, or of the pride that asserts that God would not do anything new without doing it through us. Of course, those with such a mentality are seldom used by the Lord to birth new works.

19. *They will tend to reject spiritual manifestations that they do not understand.* This is a symptom of the pride and arrogance of presuming that our opinions are the same as God's. True humility keeps us teachable and open, patiently waiting for fruit before making judgments. True discernment enables us to look for and hope for the best, not the worst. For this reason, we are exhorted to "examine everything carefully; hold

fast to that which is good" (1 Thess. 5:21, *NASB*), not to what is bad.

20. *People with the religious spirit will overreact to carnality in the Church.* The truth is, there is probably far more carnality in the Church, and a lot less of the Holy Spirit, than even the most critical person has guessed. It is important that we learn to discern between the carnal and that which is from the Holy Spirit in order to be delivered from our carnality and to grow in our submission to the Holy Spirit. But the critical person will annihilate those who may still be 60 percent carnal but who were 95 percent carnal last year. Instead, we need to recognize that people are making progress and to do what we can to help them along the way.

21. *They will overreact to immaturity in the Church.* There is an immaturity that is acceptable to the Lord. My two-year-old is immature when compared with my nine-year-old, but that is to be expected. In fact, he may be very mature for a two-year-old. The idealistic religious spirit only sees the immaturity, without considering the other important factors.

22. *They will be overly prone to view supernatural manifestations as evidence of God's approval.* This is just another form of keeping score and comparing ourselves with others. Some of Jesus' greatest miracles, such as walking on water, were seen by only a few people. He was doing His works to glorify the Father, not Himself. Those who use the evidence of miracles to promote and build their own ministries and reputations have made a serious departure from the path of life.

23. *They will be unable to join anything that they do not deem perfect or nearly perfect.* The Lord joined, and even gave His life for, the fallen human race. Such is the nature of those who abide in Him.

24. *They will be overly paranoid of the religious spirit.* We do not get free of something by fearing it, but by overcoming it with faith in Christ Jesus.

25. *They will have the tendency to glory in anything but the cross of Jesus, what He has accomplished and who He is.* If we are building our lives, ministries or churches on anything but these, we are building on a shaky foundation that will not stand.

I hope that this chapter has given you illumination about problems both in yourself and in another person or ministry. But let me warn you once again to be sure that you respond in the Holy Spirit, heeding Paul's warning to the Galatians: "Brethren, even if a man is caught in any trespass, you who are spiritual, restore such a one in a spirit of gentleness; each one looking to yourself, so that you too will not be tempted" (Gal. 6:1).

God wants us to overcome the spirit of religion! We do this primarily by keeping the main thing—loving God and loving our neighbors—the main thing.

Chapter Four

THE COUNTERFEIT KINGDOM

ROBERT HEIDLER

Robert D. Heidler, Th.M., is senior pastor of the Glory of Zion Outreach Center in Denton, Texas. A graduate of Dallas Theological Seminary, Heidler has ministered extensively in Russia and Eastern Europe. He serves on the boards of Shekinah Messianic Ministries and Pray for the Peace of Jerusalem. He and his wife, Linda, have three children.

If you are reading this book, chances are good that you have already confronted the spirit of religion! As Peter Wagner pointed out in chapter 1, the spirit of religion is not mentioned by name in Scripture, but it is no stranger to those trying to move forward in the things of God.

TWO GROUPS IN THE CHURCH

When our church first began to move into the things of the Holy Spirit, I made a startling discovery. I found that there were two very different kinds of people in our church! Some members of the church were incurably hungry for more of God. They were thrilled every time God broke through. They were anxious to receive all that God would give.

But others in the church had a very different response. They *hated* any overt manifestation of God. They did not *want* to experience God's gifts. Every time the church began to move into a new realm of the Spirit, they would rise up in vehement opposition.

Both of these groups seemed outwardly committed to the Lord. Both groups included diligent workers in the church who supported the church financially, yet some were irresistibly drawn to the presence of God, while others reacted strongly against it!

Some of this resistance may certainly be explained as a natural human aversion to change, but as time went on it became evident that some members of our church, though genuine believers, were being influenced by a spiritual power that was diametrically *opposed* to God's purposes!

Over the years, I've found that this is not unusual. In most churches and Christian organizations, we find a spiritual entity at work that has an outward façade of religiosity but that is highly resistant to the progress of God's work.

What is this spirit of religion, and what insights do the Scriptures give concerning its operation?

TRUE AND FALSE WHEAT

I believe that Matthew 13:24-30 provides a key insight into the spirit of religion. In this passage Jesus tells the parable of a farmer who planted good seed in his field. As his crop came to maturity and heads of grain began to form, the farmer discovered that an enemy had sowed *zizania* (darnel, which is a false wheat sometimes called tares) in the midst of the true.[1]

Zizania is a weed that looks so much like wheat that it is, in its early stages, indistinguishable from the real thing. The difference only becomes evident when the time comes to bear fruit. Instead of bearing edible grain, zizania produces small dark seeds that often host a poisonous fungus. So in this parable, by the time the farmer discovered the enemy's mischief, the true and counterfeit wheat were so entangled that he was forced to allow them to grow together until the harvest.

In the interpretation of this parable, Jesus explains that the wheat and zizania represent two kinds of people. The wheat represents "the sons of the kingdom" (v. 38). These men and women live as representatives of God's kingdom and produce good fruit for God!

But sown in the midst of the wheat we find zizania, identified as "the sons of the evil one" (v. 38). They are planted in the field to hinder the growth of the wheat. These sons of the evil one are not necessarily bad people. They may include genuine believers who have been seduced by the enemy to oppose God's work. In Matthew 16:23 Jesus even addressed Peter as Satan when He sensed that Peter was speaking under the influence of the enemy!

A TALE OF TWO KINGDOMS

The Bible describes two kingdoms operating in the world. The *kingdom of God* seeks to accomplish the Father's will on the earth (see Matt. 6:10), which is to bring "righteousness and peace and joy in the Holy Spirit" (Rom. 14:17).

In opposition to God's kingdom, Satan has established the *kingdom of this world*. Satan's goal is to resist the progress of God's kingdom and hinder God's plan of redemption. These kingdoms are locked in a conflict that will not end until Jesus returns.

Most Christians are familiar with the *nature* of these kingdoms, but this parable tells us something important about their *appearance*. By comparing the citizens of these kingdoms to wheat and zizania, Jesus reveals that the two groups outwardly appear to be identical. Those under Satan's influence look exactly like the sons of the Kingdom!

This flies in the face of our normal way of thinking. Most Christians assume that the sons of the Kingdom are good people who go to church, while the sons of the evil one are immoral, wicked, nasty people. Christians who accept these stereotypes feel that if they can get the nasty people in their community to become nice people and attend church, the kingdom of God has prevailed!

Jesus, however, warns that this is not the case! The whole point of His parable is that the sons of the evil one do not always *look* evil!

Satan's primary strategy against the kingdom of God is not an open manifestation of evil. Satan does not come as an ugly monster with horns and a pitchfork. He appears as an "angel of light" (2 Cor. 11:14) to deceive the saints.

This parable reveals that the sons of the evil one look just like their dad! They look *good!* Satan's strategy is not to fill the world with alcoholics, rapists and murderers. He will settle for destroying lives in those ways if that's all he can get, but his Plan A is to produce *imitations* of the sons of the Kingdom, ones who do good things but who lack a vital relationship with Jesus.

Satan's goal is to *counterfeit* God's kingdom. By offering the world a dead imitation of the true Kingdom, the devil attempts to hinder the progress of God's work by vaccinating the world against God's love! *Satan's counterfeit of God's kingdom is called religion.*

A "God's Eye View" of Religion

Many Christians wrongly assume that religion is a good thing. Some think that God has won a victory when an unbeliever "finds religion" and begins to attend church. That is a false assumption. God's goal is not to create people who are religious. His goal is to bring men and women into a relationship with Himself!

> ## God's goal is not to create people who are religious. His goal is to bring men and women into a relationship with Himself!

Many are shocked to learn that God is not particularly religious! God does not put a high value on religious activity. James 1:27 tells us that there *is* such thing as pure religion that pleases God, but surprisingly, the Bible does not usually present religious activity as a good thing in itself.

In Malachi's day, for example, the people were proud of their religiosity. They assumed that their religious rituals were pleasing to God, but God indicated He was looking for something more:

> "Oh, that one of you would shut the temple doors, so that you would not light useless fires on my altar! I am not pleased with you," says the Lord Almighty, "and I will

accept no offering from your hands" (Mal. 1:10, *NIV*).

The outward forms of religion are not what God is looking for! He would prefer that someone locks the church doors than perpetuate lifeless forms of religion!

In the New Testament, religion is denounced in the harshest of terms. In the first century, the concept of religion was epitomized by the Pharisees. Pharisees were very good people. Many people think of the Pharisees in negative terms, but if we had lived when Jesus lived, we would have viewed them as the pillars of society. They were fine, upstanding people. They studied the Bible diligently, and they took the lead in defending what was good, righteous and moral. They always went to religious services and made a point of obeying God's laws. These were men you would like your sister to marry!

WHAT JESUS THINKS

If you want to see what Jesus thinks of religion, look closely at what He said to the Pharisees! Jesus never minded "sinners." He often ate with drunkards and prostitutes. He freely extended grace to the woman caught in adultery (see John 8:11). But He reserved His harshest condemnation for the Pharisees:

> Woe to you, . . . Pharisees, you hypocrites! You travel over land and sea to win a single convert, and when he becomes one, you make him twice as much a son of hell as you are (Matt. 23:15, *NIV*).

> Woe to you, . . . Pharisees, you hypocrites! You clean the outside of the cup and dish, but inside they are full of greed and self-indulgence (v. 25, *NIV*).

Woe to you, . . . Pharisees, you hypocrites! You are like
whitewashed tombs, which look beautiful on the outside but on the inside are full of dead men's bones and
everything unclean (vv. 27-28, *NIV*).

What was Jesus' problem with the Pharisees? The Pharisees
took God's truth and turned it into a religious system! They
replaced the inner reality of a relationship with God with a system
that focused on outward appearances. The New Testament con-
sistently portrays the religiosity of the Pharisees as an evil thing!

In 1 Timothy 1:15 the apostle Paul makes a surprising statement about himself. Paul portrays himself as the "worst" of sinners (*NIV*).

What terrible sin was Paul guilty of? Was he a rapist, an alco-
holic, a thief? There is no evidence that he was guilty of any of
those things. Before he came to know Jesus, Paul was a Pharisee
of the highest order. He was meticulously careful to keep God's
law.

What did Paul do that he considered such a terrible sin? I
believe that Paul is talking about the "sin" of *Phariseeism*. Paul recognized that much of his life had been dominated by a *religiosity*
that directly opposed God's purposes. His verdict was that this was
the *worst* kind of sin! His religious Phariseeism was far more of a
threat to God's kingdom than a "lesser sin" like theft or murder!

I believe that Paul understood the evil nature of a life dominated by a spirit of religion! Those who are under the influence
of the spirit of religion are like zizania planted in a wheat field.
They hold an outward form of godliness without the power to
bear fruit. They are planted in the world to "choke out" God's
kingdom and to hinder its growth. One of the most destructive
strategies of the enemy is to instill attitudes and mind-sets
through the influence of the religious spirit.

Symptoms of the Religious Spirit

Religion is a satanic counterfeit of a relationship with God. Under the influence of the religious spirit, an individual may do the right things, but for all the wrong reasons. To follow are seven characteristics of those oppressed by the religious spirit.

1. There Is an Overemphasis on Outward Form

The religious spirit wants you to say the right words, do the right things and have the right look. There is always fear of what others will think. This brings a resistance to change and a hesitancy to try anything new. Michal, Saul's daughter and David's wife, was horrified by David's exuberant dance because it went beyond what she was used to and caused her to fear criticism by his servants (see 2 Sam. 6:14-22).

God places heart attitude above outward appearance. His goal is that whatever we do be motivated by an all-consuming love for Jesus (see Mark 12:30).

2. There Is a Sense of Condemnation and Fear

The religious spirit always condemns you if you don't "get it right." There is a continual fear of failure.

In God's kingdom, there is *mercy* for those who seek God. David was guilty of terrible sins, but he was a man after God's heart. Because he loved God, he repented and experienced forgiveness.

3. There Is an Attitude of Pride and Judgment

If you are able to keep its external standard, the religious spirit will give you a self-righteous pride in your accomplishment. You feel you are better than others, and you may become critical of those who don't measure up. When the world stereotypes Christians as mean and judgmental, that's an evidence that the spirit of religion has been at work!

In God's kingdom it's all of grace. We can never achieve God's standard, but we can always turn to Him and find mercy. There is no room for self-righteousness. As we receive grace, we walk in humility and compassion.

4. There Is an Oppressive Legalism

The religious spirit offers a legalistic system with no flexibility. It wants to produce a *method* that can replace the dynamics of a *relationship*. Under a spirit of religion you are given an artificial standard and graded by your ability to perform.

The Spirit of God leads many believers to make a prayer list and pray through it daily. As they follow the Spirit's leading, they thrive spiritually and much fruit results!

The religious spirit, on the other hand, would turn this into a legalistic method: "To be a committed Christian," it would say, "you *must* have a prayer list and pray through it *every day*!" For some people, this would be a dead work and would produce no fruit.

The Holy Spirit works with each of us individually. We need to develop sensitivity to what He is saying. As we respond to His leading, good fruit is produced. Righteousness is the joy of living to please the One we love, not an oppressive obligation.

5. There Is a Need to Figure God Out

Religion reduces God to a subject for intellectual study. The goal is to understand God and make Him predictable. It's an attempt to put God in our box. New moves of the Spirit are rejected if they don't match our understanding of how God works.

The focus of the Kingdom is not understanding God, but knowing, serving and loving Him. God is a God of infinite creativity. We can never fully understand Him, but we *can* know Him and enjoy Him forever.

6. There Is a Dependence on Self-Effort

Religion seeks to gain righteousness by self-effort and discipline. Under a system of religion, everything depends on you! The spirit of religion tells you, "You failed because you didn't try hard enough. Try harder and discipline yourself more!"

In the kingdom of God, righteousness is obtained through the Holy Spirit (see Rom. 8:4). Righteousness flows from a relationship with Him. The more we yield to Him, the more His holy character is expressed in our lives.

7. There Is an Undue Emphasis on Tradition

The religious spirit will cause you to attach great honor to the work of God in the past, while standing in opposition to His will for the present. That is what happened when a spirit caused the children of Israel to burn incense to the bronze serpent (see 2 Kings 18:4). God wants us to remember His great deeds in the past without turning them into idols.

Both God's kingdom and the counterfeit look very much the same. Both can appear to be righteous, but there is a dramatic difference. In *religion* it's all a façade. In God's *kingdom*, righteousness flows from an internal reality.

BUILDING YOUR OWN APPLE TREE

My favorite illustration of religion is the story of the counterfeit apple tree.

Let's suppose you were looking through a magazine and saw a picture of an incredibly beautiful apple tree. As you beheld its beauty, you decided, *I want a tree just like that in my backyard!*

How would you go about getting an apple tree in your yard?

One way would be to take that picture of an apple tree, have it enlarged and study it in detail. From that picture you could draw up plans for the construction of an apple tree that would look *exactly* like the one in the picture.

You would start by building the framework of trunk and branches. You would determine the right size and shape of each branch and then join them together in just the right way.

You would buy lumber and carefully carve each branch, finishing the surface to look as authentic as possible, and finally fit them together according to your plan.

When the framework is complete, you would paint it to exactly match the tree in the picture. You would purchase a vast quantity of silk leaves and carefully glue each one in place. Finally, you could go down to the grocery store and buy the best apples you could find, bring them home and hang them all over your tree.

At last, you could stand back and admire the beauty of your apple tree! If you are skilled enough at your work, it would look just like the one in the picture!

WHERE IS THE LIFE?

There is only one problem: Your apple tree has no life! It is only a dead imitation. It will never produce one apple, and any apples you hang on it will rot! That is religion. It is a human attempt to duplicate the righteousness of God by sheer ability. From a human perspective it may look good, but it does not please God.

There is a second way to get an apple tree. You could get an apple seed, which is very small and doesn't look impressive. But within that seed is *life*. You plant that seed in good soil, you water and nurture it, and from that seed will *grow* an apple tree. It may take a while; but if you continue to water and nurture it, it *will* produce apples!

That's the principle of the *Kingdom*. God wants to plant His

Spirit in the good soil of a humble and repentant heart. As a relationship with the Spirit develops, the fruit of the Spirit is manifest: love, joy, peace, patience and all the rest (see Gal. 5:22-23). The fruit of the Spirit is the *essence* of righteousness. It is the *character of Jesus* being formed in you. If the fruit of the Spirit is operating in your life, you are *automatically* keeping God's commandments (see Rom. 13:8,10). As the Spirit does His work within you, God's law is written on your heart, and the righteousness of God becomes part of your life.

Just as it takes time to grow a real apple tree, so it takes time to build a relationship with God. There are no shortcuts. There may be times of failure, but if we are truly seeking God, there is grace to cover sin.

A real apple tree may not look as perfect as the one in your picture. It may have been wounded by lightening strikes and been twisted by strong winds. But it has *life*. It is real, and it can bear fruit.

BEAUTIFUL ON THE OUTSIDE, BUT DEAD ON THE INSIDE

The Pharisees looked good. Their lives were the outward picture of perfection, but Jesus saw them as whitewashed tombs—beautiful on the outside, but dead on the inside! (See Matt. 23:27.)

On the other hand, people like Abraham, David and Peter were far from perfect, but they loved God, walked with Him and were counted as righteous.

There are two ways to get an apple tree: One comes by human effort. The other grows from an inner principle of life. But only one is real.

What makes the religious spirit evil? The religious spirit tells you that you *can* build your own apple tree. It tells you that if you say the right *words* in the right *way*, do the right *things* and have the right *look*, you will be the man or woman God wants you to be.

But it also tells you that you never have to go to God in humility to receive mercy. You never experience His grace. You conform to an external standard, but you never face the wonderful uncertainty of trying to seek His face, hear His voice and respond to His leading.

The ultimate condemnation of the religious spirit is found in Matthew 7:22-23. In the last day there will be many who say "Lord, Lord, did we not prophesy in Your name, and in Your name drive out demons and perform many miracles?" (*NIV*). Their boast is, "Lord, we did it all! We got it right! It looked good!"

Yet Jesus says, "I never knew you! Depart from me!"

Jesus says there are many who *think* they are saved but who only have religion. Religion can separate you from God for eternity!

Almost as distressing are the many that *are* saved but who are robbed of their rightful inheritance by the influence of the religious spirit. Just as Christians can be afflicted by spirits of lust, anger or infirmity, so they can also be oppressed by a spirit of religion. Many true Christians have been seduced by a spirit that gives them a religious appearance while cutting them off from the joy of knowing God. Their corporate presence in the Church is one of the primary hindrances to the progress of God's work in the earth!

Deliverance from the Religious Spirit

I believe that Matthew 13:27-30 gives us a word of caution on dealing with people who are influenced by the religious spirit. In this passage Jesus warns that there is a danger in trying to root them out! Since the religious spirit works to counterfeit the true

Kingdom, it's not always easy to tell the true from the false. In trying to root out zizania, true wheat may be harmed.

We must be cautious in accusing others of having the religious spirit! There are many who appear religious but who actually are just immature in their understanding. Someone from a legalistic background may seem "religious" to me but may actually be experiencing great freedom in the Spirit!

In trying to expose the religious spirit, we must also take care that we are not ensnared ourselves.

In trying to expose the religious spirit, we must also take care that we are not ensnared ourselves. The religious spirit will try to drive us to extremes. In confronting people who have the religious spirit, I may be driven to the opposite extreme and end up just as religious as they are!

The key to dealing with the religious spirit is to draw very close to the Holy Spirit. We must stand against the influence of this spirit with firmness and gentleness, while demonstrating the love and power that are found in a true relationship with God.

Those afflicted by the religious spirit are not our enemies! In fact, there is great *hope* for them! As a Pharisee, Saul of Tarsus was dominated by the religious spirit. He resisted the new work of God with all his might, but God had a way to set him free!

Dealing with those dominated by religion requires great patience. Those who are influenced by the religious spirit are highly resistant to change because they are *convinced* that they are doing the will of God. The lie that the spirit tells them is that God *likes* their religious activity, that He is *pleased* by mere outward performance.

But when the grace of God breaks through and individuals experience the life of God, they can be set free!

SET YOURSELF FREE!

In the introduction to my book *Experiencing the Spirit*, I share how I grew up in a Bible-believing home, served on the staff of a leading evangelical ministry and graduated from a leading evangelical seminary. I strongly resisted the work of the Holy Spirit, but I was convinced that I was right. I knew all the theological arguments to defend my position! I was good and moral and proud. In short, I was a *Pharisee*. Then the Holy Spirit fell; and literally, overnight (without my asking) I was baptized in the Holy Spirit and spoke in tongues.

The night before I was inundated by God's grace, a close friend had a very strange word for me. He said, "I see that you are looking at everything through a stained-glass window [symbolizing religion] and can't see clearly. But God's going to do something, and you will see."

Several hours later, while I slept, God smashed the stained-glass window! He set me free from the religious spirit that had kept me in bondage and brought me out into the joy of a relationship with Him.

If you feel that you are bound or inhibited by the spirit of religion, you undoubtedly need deliverance. You can go to a respected deliverance minister and seek help. Before you do that, however, you may want to read my book *Set Yourself Free!* In it I explain how God has given individuals the authority and the spiritual power to confront and overcome a considerable number of personal demonic afflictions, including bondage to the spirit of religion, through self-deliverance.

Whether through self-deliverance or through the ministry of another, modern-day Pharisees *can* be set free! By prayer, intercession and the manifestation of God's love, the stained-glass windows of religion can be broken. I repeat: Those afflicted by the religious spirit are not the enemy. The bright light of God's grace can be released to shine on them as it did on Saul of Tarsus. Let God give you faith to see yourself and other captives set free—even from the spirit of religion!

Chapter Five

PERSONAL FREEDOM FROM THE SPIRIT OF RELIGION

E. LEO LAWSON, JR.

After graduating from the University of Kentucky with a degree in education, Leo Lawson began what has now become over 25 years of campus ministry. When he began vocational ministry in Michigan, Leo met and married his wife, Patricia. For over 10 years, Leo and Patricia pastored a community church while directing campus life at Michigan State University. Later they ministered on campuses in Texas and California.

Presently, Leo is the dean of Victory Campus Ministries' Graduate School of Campus Ministry. This school, in league with Fuller Seminary, is training cross-cultural campus missionaries. Together, Leo and Patricia have trained over 300 campus missionaries in the United States and in countries around the world.

Leo is also the academic dean for Victory Club's Graduate School of Youth Ministry. In addition to his responsibilities with these graduate schools, Leo is a teacher for Victory Leadership Institute, which is based in his local church, Every Nation Christian Church of Palos Verdes. He serves in the city government in Rancho Palos Verdes, California. He is on the board of the Apostolic Council for Educational Accountability and continues to be an adjunct professor for Fuller Seminary's Missions Department. Leo Lawson currently has a master's degree in intercultural studies from Fuller Seminary and is working on his doctorate in missiology.

Pastor Leo and Patricia have been married for 22 years, and together they are the dedicated parents of three teenagers: Joshua, Jeremy and Julianne.

I had a hunger for God at a very early age. Walking around on my grandfather's Kentucky farm, I would talk to Jesus just as loudly as I would talk to anyone else. Why? Because I sensed His presence. However, I did not know *Him*. It was like sitting in the audience of a president—you *experience* his presence, though you know him not.

My grandfather, a Baptist deacon, would sit me on his knee and read his Bible to me. Inquiring soul that I was, I wanted to know much about this Jesus whose presence I so sensed, as children often do. My Catholic mother would take me, along with my Baptist dad, to Mass; and then in the next hour, she would attend the Baptist service with my father and me. This worked fine until the priest demanded that our commitment be to the Catholic Church, not to the Baptist Church, if I was going to attend their parochial Catholic school.

SEARCHING FOR GOD

When I entered the first of eight years of Catholic grade school, I certainly carried with me this hunger for God. After hearing the Ten Commandments and all the requirements to participate in the Mass, I set my mind and heart to "do the dos," and "don't the don'ts." I figured that if that was how to please the God whose presence I so treasured, then that was what I would pursue with all my juvenile might.

Yet sometime just past my First Communion, the years of devotion to "religion" seemed to drain away the sense of God's presence. The very God I wanted to know seemed ever so far, so intensifying my *commitment* appeared to be the only remedy. Being an altar boy was attractive to me. I even checked out Catholic seminaries in the seventh and eighth grades, hoping that the priesthood might be the place to find God—but to no avail. Where was He? At graduation I decided that there was no reality in "religion," though my earlier experience with the Baptists left me wondering whether there was something more than what the Catholics were telling me.

My experience of "the priesthood" during my school years left a bad aftertaste. No, there was no clergy sex abuse. But I would propose that something at least as damaging occurred in my young soul during those years. The spirit of religion dulled the sense of God's presence within me *and* nullified God's Word to me. Should this surprise you? It shouldn't, because this is exactly what Jesus said it would do.

JESUS EXPOSED THE SPIRIT OF RELIGION

Jesus rebuked the religious leaders of His day, telling them that they could not discern when God was present, even when standing there in human flesh! (See John 8.) What was it that Jesus discerned about the Pharisees' religious past that had so dulled them to God's presence? Of all the religious sects in His day, Jesus would have probably most aligned Himself with what the Pharisees taught, yet His harshest rebukes came their way. Why? There was nothing so wrong about what they *said* as there was about what they *did* (see Matt. 23:3). There was just something about the spirit behind their words and deeds that made them detestable, especially to God. They professed to know Him, but by their deeds they denied God (see Titus 1:16). Like so many religious people, their words seemed right, but these folks did not have a right spirit. Could this have been caused by a demonic spirit?

AKA: The Religious Spirit

Some people would call it the spirit of religion; and others, the spirit of religiosity. One names a spirit by the destiny it distributes over someone; i.e., the spirit of religiosity distributes that demonic destiny. However, it might more simply be called the religious spirit. Lest we damn all "religion," I must make clear that religion can be human initiated, and some of it can even be good. "To keep oneself unstained by the world" (Jas. 1:27, *NASB*) is self-initiated, though only made possible by God's grace.

However, in God's sight, religion can be "pure and undefiled" (Jas. 1:27). Therefore it must also be possible for religion to be impure and defiled. One source of that defiled religion is a demonic spirit of religiosity. This seems to be what Jesus discerned to be at work when He was around most Pharisees. In Matthew 15:1-9, Jesus uncovered the root of their religious spirit, as we shall see.

Prior to His exposé on religiosity, Jesus had returned from Gennesaret, where the sick folks were simply touching His garment and getting healed (see Matt. 14:34-36). But such manifest power is where the rub came. Just like today, it seems that the perpetrators of "religion" just couldn't tolerate the power of God flowing so readily. The central motivating factor behind the religious spirit is pride in its self-righteous works, and this, too, was what was welling up inside of those Pharisees. They felt that Jesus was showing them up! So they determined to shut down such a "show" of power in order to secure their own position in society. The religious spirit never changes. It still shows up that way today!

As those vultures circled around the Master, they could find no fault with Him. So they turned their attention to His rough-hewn disciples, who cared little for "religion" over reality—heaven's reality brought to the earth by the power of God's king-dom. Offended, the Pharisees fixed their gaze on these men and, yes, found that they violated the traditions of the elders. The disciples did not wash their hands according to the ceremonial tra-ditions, and, thus, these renegades did not qualify with the Pharisees.

> Then some Pharisees and scribes came to Jesus from Jerusalem and said, "Why do Your disciples break the tradition of the elders? For they do not wash their hands when they eat bread." And He answered and said to them, "And do you yourselves transgress the command-ment of God for the sake of your tradition?" (Matt. 15:1-3, *NASB*).

Dethroning the Traditions from Men

The Twelve were mostly outdoorsmen. Jesus' leading disciples were fishermen. Eating without washing their hands, well, that's just life! But not so for these Pharisees. The tradition of the elders had spoken—*this* was a mortal sin! Jewish legend had it that these traditions orally came down from Moses, but the Hebrew Torah (the Law), which Moses received from God, said nothing about pre-meal hand washing. However, it did say that nothing was to be taken away or added to the Torah (see Deut. 4:2).

In truth, over the years Jewish priests had simply added their own oral commentary (the Talmud) and made dogma of it. Their religious dogma was so twisted that it violated God's commands. Their dogma was for the dogs! The oral traditions were not even written down until the time of the Romans, over 1,000 years after Moses. Why then should these Talmud proclamations be given the same weight as the Torah, which God gave to Moses on the mountain? By extension, what does this suggest about the place of church dogma that is contradicted by the Scripture?

As usual, Jesus goes right to the heart of the issue. For these Pharisees, traditions from men had taken *priority* over God's Word! May I suggest to you that this is the root of the religious spirit? When this happens, God's Word does not just get undervalued—Jesus said that it gets nullified, or invalidated (see Matt. 15:6). The New Testament Greek word for "nullified" derives from *kuros*, which means "supremacy," and thus implies lordship.[1] Jesus was saying that the lordship of God's Word had been annulled by choosing traditions from men over His Word. Consider the power of God's word that created the ever-expanding universe. Yet with one choice, that power can be nullified in a person's life!

HOW A RELIGIOUS SPIRIT IS RECEIVED

How then does a religious spirit obtain a legal right into your life? Human-initiated religion finds its way into the fabric of a society and becomes a tradition passed on to you. But the source is human, and it is properly called traditions from men. When the status quo exalts such tradition over God's command, the status quo has to go. But the status quo dies hard; when a person individually chooses to make traditions from men the priority, the religious spirit has found a legal right and can demonize the soul of that person. Demons find access to the soul through all deeds of the flesh, and religion can sometimes be no more than simply a deed of the flesh, when it is not rooted in a relationship with God.

Working in evangelism to win religious people over the years, I have found that the first thing I have to do, especially with religious folks, is to ask them if the Word of God is *the* priority with them. "If, for some reason, your religious tradition is found to be in contradiction with God's Scripture, will the Word of God be your final authority?" I ask. Only when this is affirmed can I go further in ministry with them. This decision weakens the right of the religious spirit to their soul, and the stronghold of the religious spirit begins to crumble.

However, Jesus said that if an unsaved religious person chooses to hold to man-made traditions, it becomes an act of "neglecting the commandment of God" (Mark 7:8, *NASB*). The Greek word for "neglect" here is the same word that Paul used to speak of a man's divorcing his wife (see 1 Cor. 7:11-12).[2] In other words, when you choose traditions from men as a top priority, you end up divorcing yourself from God's Word. This gives ground to the religious spirit.

Jesus attacked the root of the spirit of religion in these Pharisees. He illustrated how, by their tradition keeping, God's commandment had been transgressed, that is, side-stepped (see Matt. 15:3). Yes, the Greek word for "transgress" also means "to overstep, neglect, violate," namely God's laws.[3] Accordingly, a transgression occurs when one sidesteps the basics of the faith.

This is a manifestation of the religious spirit. It causes a person to give more attention to the *application* of a principle than to the principle itself. *Both* are important, but the weightier provisions of God's laws (principles) are to have the priority (see Matt. 23:23). Principle is principal! A religious spirit moves a person away from the basics, and something else comes into focus. The basics fade into the background and external ritual wins the day.

RITUAL – RELATIONSHIP = RELIGION

Jesus characterized the byproduct of the religious spirit: ritual without relationship. External ritual is hollow without an internal relationship with God. According to Jesus, this is the real meaning of the word "hypocrite." The word Jesus used originally came from Greek theater. When used negatively, it referred to actors who did not identify themselves with their roles. From this came its meanings of "play-acting," "disguise" and "hypocrisy."[4] Hypocrites, then, are not the same on the inside as they are on the outside. This is another manifestation of the religious spirit! People who yield to it too often lack integrity, or simply put, are hypocrites. Hypocrites are what Jesus called the Pharisees, pointing out that Isaiah had prophesied of their kind 700 years earlier. Thus Jesus dynamically quotes Isaiah 29:13:

> By this you invalidated the word of God for the sake of your tradition. You hypocrites, rightly did Isaiah prophesy of you: "This people honors Me with their lips, but their heart is far away from Me. But in vain do they worship Me, teaching as doctrines the precepts of men" (Matt. 15:6-9, *NASB*; see also Mark 7:6-9,13).

They had ritual without relationship.

HOW DO YOU RATE?

Though the sect of the Pharisees did not exist in Isaiah's day, Jesus still said that Isaiah prophesied about their kind. Jesus identified some of the hallmarks of these hypocrites as those same hallmarks that Isaiah used to describe such religious people of his day (see Matt. 15:1-9; Mark 7:1-13). Let's look at Jesus and Isaiah's description of the effects of the spirit of religion.

1. You focus more on the externals, rather than focusing *first* on being right internally. The Pharisees whose hearts were far from God asked Jesus, "Why do Your disciples . . . eat their bread with impure hands?" (Mark 7:5, *NASB*).

2. You are a hypocrite: one thing on the outside, but another within. Jesus said, "[Hypocrites] honor Me with their lips, but their heart is far away from Me" (Mark 7:6, *NASB*).

3. You sidestep the basic *principles*, focusing more on their application. Jesus responded to the Pharisees' question with another question: "Why do you yourselves transgress [sidestep] the commandment of God for the sake of your tradition [application]?" (Matt. 15:3, *NASB*).

4. You prioritize (or make equal) tradition from men *alongside* of God's Word. Because the Pharisees refused to follow God's commands, Jesus said to them, "By this you invalidated the word of God for the sake of your tradition" (Matt. 15:6, *NASB*).

5. You *accuse* those who do not exalt your tradition (i.e., any church dogma). The Pharisees asked, "Why do Your disciples break the tradition of the elders? For they do not . . ." (Matt. 15:2, *NASB*).

6. You divorce yourself from God's Word, *dismissing* its lordship over you. Jesus responded with a number of true accusations: "Neglecting [dismissing the lordship of] the commandment of God, you hold to the tradition of men" (Mark 7:8, *NASB*).

7. You *set aside* [reject] God's Word in order to practice traditions from men. "You are experts at setting aside the commandment of God in order to keep your tradition" (Mark 7:9, *NASB*).

8. You invalidate God's Word by practicing traditions from men and doing so regularly. "Thus invalidating the word of God by your tradition . . . ; and you do many things such as that" (Mark 7:13, *NASB*).

9. You have ritual, not relationship with God! "Their heart is far away from Me. But in vain do they worship Me" (Mark 7:6-7, *NASB*).

10. You falsely honor God with your lips, while holding your *heart* far from Him. "This people honors Me with their lips, but their heart is far away from Me" (Mark 7:6, *NASB*).

11. You worship with *empty* words; your heart is not engaged behind the words. "Their heart is far away from Me. But in vain do they worship Me" (Mark 7:6-7, *NASB*).

12. You accept as your *code of conduct* traditions from men, and not God's precepts. "Teaching as doctrines the precepts of men" (Mark 7:7, *NASB*).

THE REASON JUDGMENT COMES

Even though human authority enforced religious ritual, Isaiah 29 makes it clear that when those hypocrites chose ritual over relationship in their worship, God still held them responsible for their *choice*. In fact, the *first* word the Lord used in verse 13 was "because." Thus He gave the reason for the judgment that He had poured out on the people who had made that choice—*heartless worship*.

> Because this people draw near with their words and honor Me with their lip service, but they remove their hearts far from Me, and their reverence for me consists of tradition learned by rote, therefore behold, I will once again *deal* . . . (Isa. 29:13-14, *NASB*, emphasis added).

Like the Pharisees of Jesus' day, the hypocrites of Isaiah's day were one thing on the outside, but inside they distanced themselves from God—and it showed up in their worship. Heartless worship is a stench in the nostrils of God and thus God deals out judgment to this kind of worshiper, who is under the influence of a religious spirit.

THE INTOXICATION OF RELIGION

So let's look at the hand that God *dealt* to those who yielded to a religious spirit. Just three verses earlier, God began to sentence them, saying, "Be delayed and wait, blind yourselves and be blind; they become drunk, but not with wine, they stagger, but not with strong drink. The wisdom of their wise men will perish, and the discernment of their discerning men will be concealed" (vv. 9,14). That is to say, "Stop dead in your tracks and gawk, as with a drunken stare; be amazed and ponder God's Word, yet in the end you will *not* understand with your mind what God is trying to reveal to you." It is as if you were in a darkened room, and suddenly the brilliance of the strongest camera flash enters your eyes and blinds you so that you can't see, though you look intently.

This is the blindness that comes upon those who yield to the religious spirit. Put simply, this spirit causes you to "blind yourself" when trying to look at God and His Word. Thus, you look right past Him and His Word. Some theologians have called this spiritual drunkenness. It is an intoxication with *religious ritual* that short-circuits an intimate relationship with God. Heartless lip service produces a self-induced hardening of the heart.

This religious hardening makes the senses numb more than any intoxication that wine could ever achieve. This is a dulling of your spiritual senses. You just don't "feel" what others get from God. You stagger from place to place, hoping you will find something that connects you to God; but to your dismay you bounce from one wall to another, from one church to another, hoping to find something to awaken you from this lifeless stupor. Your heartless ritual has left you bankrupt and in a drunken state that compromises your morals, as you spiral ever downward with a hopeless religion that doesn't deliver.

A SPIRIT OF STUPOR

For [Because] the LORD has poured over you a spirit of deep sleep, He has shut your eyes, the prophets; and He has covered your heads, the seers. The entire vision will be to you like the words of a sealed book, which when they give it to the one who is literate, saying, "Please read this," he will say, "I cannot, for it is sealed." Then the book will be given to one who is illiterate, saying, "Please read this." And he will say, "I cannot read" (Isa. 29:10-12).

There's that word again: "because." Why did all this spiritual debauchery, or drunkenness, occur? Because each person chose ritual over relationship. As a result, a *demonic* spirit of stupor was poured over those who chose their own religious works above God's commands (see v. 13). This is the source of that dullness and drunkenness.[5] According to Keil and Delitzsch, "this stupefaction was the self-inflicted punishment of the dead works with which the people mocked God and deceived themselves."[6]

God abhors empty worship; heartless words only mock Him. Because of the choices these people made, God permitted a spirit of stupor to be poured over these people. The original Hebrew text calls it a spirit of *tardemah,* meaning "trance" or "deep sleep."[7] This spirit would hypnotize a person into a drunken stare, under the influence, staggering throughout their religious days, insensible and impervious to God's Spirit of revelation and His Word. This hypnotic spirit was so poured out on them that they were drenched, baptized, immersed and drowning in their own religious ritual. The eyes of their heart were shut, so they could not catch the nation's prophetic direction—the vision from God eluded them (see v. 10).

People with this spirit to whom I have ministered can never seem to catch the vision of Christ's Church or hear the prophetic word of the Lord. I ministered to one prophet who, when he was also vexed by a religious spirit, would bounce in and out of his prophetic gift. When he was on prophetically, he was really on. But when this religious spirit attacked him, he could hardly discern any nudging from God's Spirit. As verse 10 describes, "He has shut your eyes, the prophets."

Under the Influence of the Spirit of Stupor

As Isaiah 29:14 explains, the result of this punishment was the loss of wisdom and discernment. Why? They made the choice, and thus a spirit of stupor was poured out on them and hypnotized them. The words used in this verse "signify the powerless, passive state of utter spiritual insensibility."[8] *This is the religious spirit* that locks people into passivity and the status quo—spirit of stupefaction. It is a stupidity that drives one to madness against God's Word, thus nullifying it. That is what happens to people with the spirit of stupor—they are driven mad against the Word, especially the Word made flesh. Doesn't it seem to be more than a few religious theologians out there? This spirit of stupor can harden their hearts and make them hardheaded, too!

The Spirit of Stupor Is a Demon
Religiosity gives the spirit of stupor the right to take up occupancy in a person. Dare we call this a demonic spirit? Kasemann asserts, "Israel's inability to see salvation has a demonic depth which resists the Spirit of God. . . . In the righteousness of *works* there comes into effect th[is] power . . . the immanent power of the cosmos which comes to a peak in religiosity. . . . The Lord and demons are most sharply opposed at this point. It is here that blindness and deafness arise most easily" (emphasis added).[9] Yes, this spirit of stupor is a demonic spirit that "benumb[s] the faculties, and make[s] them insensible."[10] But why do I call it the spirit of stupor instead of the spirit of deep sleep, as translated in Isaiah 29?

The Spirit of Stupor and Its Results

> But if [God's choice of us] is by grace, it is no longer on the basis of works, otherwise grace is no longer grace. What then? What Israel is seeking, it has not obtained, but those who were chosen obtained it, and the rest were hardened; just as it is written, "God gave them a spirit of

stupor, eyes to see not and ears to hear not, down to this
very day" (Rom. 11:6-8, *NASB*).

In Romans 11:8, Paul dynamically quoted the phrase "a spirit of
deep sleep" from Isaiah 29:10 and translated it as "a spirit of stupor." He explained that he, and those like him, had received grace
by faith and that those Israelites who sought that grace by works of
righteousness *did not* receive it. Their heartless religious works produced an external religiosity that brought on them a spirit of stupor, which hardened them (see vv. 5-7). This was just as it is today
with many Jews and other such religious people. As Kasemann
notes, "Not sins, but pious works prevent Judaism from obtaining
the salvation held out to it, and keep it in bondage."[11]

Then, in verses 8 and 9, Paul amplified Isaiah's description
of those who are under the power of the demonic spirit of stupor. The insensibility and hardness showed themselves in lives
lived according to their appetites. It was not that their senses
were starved of God's things, but rather that they were inundated with the *wrong* things, things that fed into their appetites.
"The torpor [stupor] seems the result of too much sensation,
dulled by incitement into apathy," explains Robinson.[12] Those
professing "saints" were so dull to God that they flooded their
senses with what their appetites demanded, only to be *further*
dulled. They're the kind that you might find in the back seat of
a car in the church parking lot after a church service, being
immoral with one of their fellow youth group members, while
earlier in church, they pretended to worship. They're also the
kind that might swindle a client out of millions of dollars,
though the previous day at church spoke piously of righteousness. These two people have different appetites, but both are following their appetites all the same.

From the days of Moses, through the days of Isaiah and

Jesus, down to Paul's day and our own, this spirit of stupor has hardened those who rendered to God only external lip service while they held their hearts far from Him. The spirit of stupor hardens the heart, blinds the eyes and deafens the ears to God. Of this hardness, Albert Barnes explains, "It comes from a word which signifies properly to become *hard*, as bones do which are broken and are then united; or as the joints sometimes do when they become callous or stiff. It was probably applied also to the formation of a hard substance in the eye, a cataract; and then means the same as to be blinded. Hence, applied to the mind, it means that which is *hard, obdurate, insensible, stupid*" (emphasis added).[13] This is that hardness of heart that we too often see among young people and adults alike.

HAS DEAD RELIGION LEFT YOU BANKRUPT?

A religious person you might be, but defiled religion only defiles you and leaves you bankrupt. According to Romans 11:8-9, your appetites snare you, trap you, stumble you, judge you, blind you and enslave you. Does Paul's description of a religious person who is under the influence of a spirit of stupor fit you? How do you rate yourself now? Here are Paul's additional descriptors of such a religious person:

1. You are always *seeking* grace and victory (redemption) but never obtaining them. "What Israel is seeking, it has not obtained" (Rom. 11:7, *NASB*).
2. You do works of righteousness but never *sense* God's acceptance. "There has also come to be at the present time a remnant *according to God's gracious choice. . . . It is not longer on the basis of works*" (Rom. 11:5-6, *NASB*, emphasis added).

3. You sense that the grace you were seeking at church always *eludes* you after the service is over. "On the basis of works, . . . what Israel is seeking, it has not obtained" (Rom. 11:6-7, *NASB*).

4. You go to church, but you leave *more* dulled (hardened) than before you came. "The rest were hardened" (Rom. 11:7, *NASB*)

5. You "see not" and "hear not" what *other* saints get out of the pastor's message. "Eyes to see not and ears to hear not" (Rom. 11:8, *NASB*).

6. You are lured by your appetites and lusts *away* from obedience to God. "Let their table become a snare and a trap, and a stumbling block" (Rom. 11:9, *NASB*).

7. You feel so enslaved to sin that your *back* will be bent forever (i.e., that you'll never change). "Let their eyes be darkened to see not, and bend their backs forever" (Rom. 11:10, *NASB*).

Does this description somewhat describe you? It certainly described my life for years after I met the Lord—that is, until I got delivered from a religious spirit! It seemed that all the talk of a victorious Christian life was *just talk* and could never be a reality for me. My back was bent with slavery to sin, lusts and appetites that chased me into a corner. The more I heard the preacher say, the more dulled and despairing I became. I was always seeking for the grace to win, but it forever slipped through my hands like sand. *Could God ever be pleased with me?* I wondered.

Though slow in coming, the day of my deliverance arrived. My pastor helped me see the effects that this demon, which he called a religious spirit, had on my life. He charged me to take responsibility for the choices I had made before and after becoming a Christian. Once that spirit was cast out, it was as if a veil were lifted from my eyes. I could then hear the Word of God in a way that brought permanent transformation in my character. The spirit of revelation (see Eph. 1:17) replaced the spirit of religion, and life with God became a joy—relationship, not ritual!

How to Receive Deliverance

As you have been reading this book, if you have experienced an inner feeling that the spirit of religion might have more of a grip on you than you would like, there is hope.

You can be set free from a spirit of religiosity. But you must be willing to take responsibility for the choice you previously made to exalt traditions from men above God's Word. You undoubtedly chose a heartless religion over relationship with God at some point in your past. It may have been when your mother admonished you to "practice your religion" so that you would not disappoint your grandma. But it's more likely that you made your decision at a more formal occasion, like Confirmation, where you exercised your own volitional abilities. In that moment, you made an alliance with external religion apart from a right relationship with God. You rendered lip service, but your self-centered heart was still far from God. For me this occurred at my First Communion.

If you decide to renounce this alliance with such religion, you should forever repent of trying to appease God with your external rituals, thinking that you are paying Him off so that He will leave you alone to do your own desires. No! Instead you should turn from being your own lord to allow Christ to be your Lord. Then make a covenant to obey, by grace, God's Word as your final authority. Renounce any man-made traditions that stand contrary to His Word. Finally, renounce your agreement with that demon called the spirit of religion to which you gave legal ground through your sin of exalting the traditions from men above God and His Word.

Then ask someone in authority over your life, like a parent or pastor, to verbally break the power of this ungodly alliance with such religion, affirming only your covenant with Christ. That person needs to agree with you, asking for God to forgive your sin of idolizing such traditions over God's Word. That person should pray for your mind, emotions and will to be healed and cleansed from this unrighteousness (see 1 John 1:7). When you renounce your alliance with the spirit of religiosity, this person with spiritual authority over you will cancel all the legal rights of that spirit and will bind it and cast it out of your soul and body. Lastly, pray together with this person, asking the Holy Spirit to flow out of your innermost being (your spirit) like a river of living water and to fill every area of your soul that the spirit of religiosity had once afflicted.

Congratulations! Now make sure that by faith you *engage* your heart each time you open your mouth in the service of your worship of God (see Heb. 13:15)!

SAMPLE PRAYERS

Here is an example of a prayer that you can pray:

Father in heaven, I love You with all my heart. I repent for the times I chose ritual over relationship with You. Specifically, I renounce the alliance with vain religion that I have made. I will now engage my heart regularly when I pray and worship You. Your Word is the final authority in my life. I will no longer

exalt man-made traditions over Your Word. Jesus, I ask You to
cleanse me from this sin. I receive Your forgiveness by faith in
the blood of Your cross. I now renounce this spirit of religion. I
yield to the Holy Spirit that I might worship in spirit and truth.
In the name of Jesus I pray, amen.

Here is an example of a prayer to be spoken over you by your
spiritual authority:

Father in heaven, I thank You for bringing [your name]
into relationship with You. As this child of God has repented
of [his/her] *vain religious practices, I thank You for*
forgiving and cleansing [him/her] *from any unrighteousness.*
As [he/she] *has renounced* [his/her] *alliance with*
vain religion, I break this alliance and its power by the
authority of Jesus Christ. In the name of Jesus Christ,
I command you, Spirit of Religion, to attention and I render
you powerless. I cancel all of your alliances with any other
demons and I cancel all your rights to [your name]*'s soul.*
I now command you to leave [him/her] *and never enter*
again. Now in its place, I ask that the Spirit of God come and
fill [your name]. *Thank You, Father, for setting* [your name]
free! In the name of Jesus I pray, amen!

Chapter Six

PROTECTING YOUR SOUL FROM THE SPIRIT OF RELIGION

TOMMI FEMRITE

Tommi Femrite is an apostolic missionary to the nations. As a spiritual strategist, Tommi is able to assess the enemy's grip, receive God's strategic battle plans and communicate these plans to leaders with great precision, thus empowering them to dismantle demonic strongholds and push back forces of darkness. Her proficiency and accuracy in the prophetic have brought international acclaim. Tommi's passion for Jesus radiates as she teaches and ministers, thus creating in the hearts of her hearers a desire to know Him more intimately.

As cofounder and president of the international ministry Gate-Keepers International, Tommi helps identify, train and encourage spiritual gatekeepers and watchmen in churches, families, businesses, schools, governments and parachurch ministries. This is done through teaching, training, empowering and giving prophetic insight. Tommi ministers on local, regional, national and international levels. More than 30 nations have received a deposit of God's glory in their lands through her ministry.

In addition to coauthoring Intercessors: Discover Your Prayer Power, *Tommi has authored* Praying with Passion: Life-Changing Prayers for Those Who Walk in Darkness, *a powerful resource for those called to pray for the lost. Tommi is an ordained minister, has earned a Doctorate of Practical Ministry from Wagner Leadership Institute and is a member of both the International Coalition of Apostles and the Eagles' Vision Apostolic Team. Tommi and her husband, Ralph, live in Colorado Springs, Colorado. They have two grown children and four grandchildren.*

Reach out and catch the truth that you are about to receive in this chapter as though God were throwing you a lifeline that would change you forever and thrust you into the fullness of your destiny. When you catch it, the spirit of religion won't be able to quench the fire that burns within you, nor will it keep you from God's plans as it desires to do.

THE BATTLE FOR MY SOUL

There was a time in my life when I was more interested in what people thought than what God thought. Oh, I may have said I was interested in what God thought, but my actions proved otherwise. Much to my amazement I realized that I was bound by a religious spirit. What followed was a journey to discover how this spirit not only operated in my life and moved through other people but also had power over me. I soon realized that the battle was over my soul—my mind, my will and my emotions.

During my quest, I discovered the religious spirit's agenda and many of its hidden plans. My freedom soon followed! You can walk in this freedom, too. The religious spirit attacks us in our minds and moves through people like you and me, if given an opportunity. It operates through Christians and non-Christians alike, because it is no respecter of persons.

THE RELIGIOUS SPIRIT'S MODI OPERANDI

During the Vietnam war, American pilots were often shot down within their first 10 combat missions. To remedy the situation, the United States Air Force authorized the formation of aggressor squadrons. Their mission was to fly, think, respond and fight like the enemy in a plane similar to the enemy's. My husband, Ralph, commanded the Pacific aggressor squadron. Ralph's squadron flew a minimum of 10 dogfights against each of our American pilots in the Pacific. Knowing how the enemy thought, operated, responded and fought made a tremendous difference in the success of our pilots also during the Gulf wars. You can apply these same principles in the spirit realm and succeed in protecting your soul from the religious spirit.

What is the religious spirit and how will I recognize it? you may be wondering. Even though the religious spirit is an ancient spirit, it's not as ancient as the Ancient of Days! Some refer to it as the Pharisee spirit, but it existed long before the Pharisees. You will recognize the religious spirit by its modi operandi, which have not changed since this spirit began its operation.

Counterfeits the Expression of God

Satan has a counterfeit for everything the Lord has. If you know anything about counterfeit money, you know that there are excellent counterfeits that take an expert to detect. But there are also poor counterfeits that just about anyone could detect. Sometimes when the religious spirit begins to attack, you will know immediately that it is the religious spirit. Other times you are going to need someone who is grounded in the Word and who walks in greater discernment. This person will be able to look at it and say, "This is close to being like God, close to being like the Holy Spirit, close to being like Jesus—but there is *just enough difference* to realize that it is not God."

Denies God's Word and Character

The spirit of religion manifested itself back in the Garden of Eden when Satan came to Adam and Eve to question them and put doubt in their minds regarding what God had really said about eating the fruit of the trees in the Garden (see Gen. 3:1-5). Likewise, it wants you to question, doubt and deny the Word of God. "Deny" is defined as "to state that something declared or believed to be true is not true; to refuse to recognize or acknowledge; to repudiate—reject as having no authority or binding force."[1]

The religious spirit would like you to believe that what God said yesterday has no authority or binding force for today. This is a lie straight from the pit of hell. God's Word will accomplish that which it says it will do, and it will not return void. His Word stands forever! (See Isa. 40:8; 55:11.)

Perhaps you have received a prophetic word that has yet to be fulfilled. This spirit puts doubt in your mind as to whether God really spoke to you. If it can get you to deny one prophetic word, then it may even get you to deny all the prophetic words spoken over your life. Sometimes we believe in our heads what God says, but when it comes right down to our hearts, we don't believe Him.

Have you ever whined before the Lord and said, "I am all

alone. No one cares about me. No one even knows I am here"? The religious spirit will have you think that God has abandoned you or that He doesn't even know your name or that He may know your name but He doesn't care about you any more, since He has left you all alone to fend for yourself. But don't be deceived. This is *not* God's character. God does *not* do or say things like this.

Shield your soul from the enemy's lies by choosing to believe what you say you believe. Counter every lie of the enemy with truth. Search the Scriptures for what God has to say concerning the lie. For example, take the lie "God has abandoned me." God says, "I will never leave you nor forsake you. I will never abandon you. I am with you *always*" (see Josh. 1:5; Deut. 4:31; Matt. 28:20). Acknowledge God's Word as true and affirm that God is bound by His Word to honor His Word. Set yourself in agreement with His Word. And when in doubt, call on Jesus—He is the truth (see John 14:6).

Upholds Tradition over Truth
Those bound by the spirit of religion choose to uphold tradition rather than truth. They feel so comfortable in the way things have always been in their personal lives or in the Church that they are not open to the new things God is doing. God says, "Behold, I will do something new, now it will spring forth; will you not be aware of it?" (Isa. 43:19, *NASB*).

If you respond, "No, I don't want something new; I like the old way," then you may be bound by the religious spirit. You pray for God to take you higher, but as soon as He begins, you cry out, "I want to go back!" This is the spirit of religion, which causes you to honor tradition more than you honor God and His Word and which keeps you from going forward with the Lord.

Validates Hypocrisy

My family was living in the Philippines when my daughter was 15 years old. I had been a Christian for three years. One day we were having a mother-daughter argument, when she yelled, "I hate you! I hate what you stand for! I hate who you are! You're a hypocrite!" Her words went like arrows into my heart. I knew that she was right—I was a hypocrite. You see, I could stand before a group of women or a congregation and look so spiritual, sound so wise and act the part.

However, I wasn't the same person in my home as I was outside the house. In fact, I thought I could relax and let my flesh hang out when I was at home. God showed me through the words of my daughter that I was using my home as a place to validate my sin. My home was a place where I could be angry, judgmental, critical and rude.

Sin was so much a part of my life before I became a Christian that it took time for the Lord to change my wrongful responses, my sinful behavior and my heart. I am so grateful that my daughter spoke those words to me, because it caused me to go before the Lord and ask, "Okay God, where doesn't my life line up?" Looking back now, I realize that I was being victimized by the spirit of religion. This religious spirit deceives you into thinking that the outward details of your behavior are what counts, not what is deep in your heart. It makes you a hypocrite.

Appeals to Your Flesh

The religious spirit was behind the devil when he appeared to Jesus in the desert and tried to get Jesus to worship him (see Luke 4:5-7). This spirit will offer you things that appeal to your pride and self-worth, and tempt you to compromise. Let's look at just a few of its tactics.

The religious spirit will cause you to walk in pride rather than in humility. Humility is acknowledging that you're able to do what you do only because God empowers, anoints and calls you. Many of us have been taught that when we say good things about ourselves, it's prideful. But I believe that when you say the good things about yourself that God says about you, it's not pride—it's humility.

You need to agree with God. Perhaps the Lord has been telling you that you are a mighty child of God. If your response is, "Oh no, Lord, not me!" it may sound like humility, but actually it's pride. In reality you are saying that you know more than God does in this particular situation. When you begin to deny or speak against what God says about you, it's as though you were saying that God doesn't really know who you are. This is the religious spirit putting thoughts in your mind. God not only knows who you are, but He also knows what He wants you to be in the future. Start agreeing with what God says about you, and you will defeat the religious spirit.

The spirit of religion justifies itself. Do you ever justify your wrong behavior by blaming someone who has hurt you or ignored you or mistreated you? When you justify your sin like that, you're trying to make yourself look good, and it becomes another form of pride. When you don't admit that you are wrong and you blame others for your sin, you are yielding to the religious spirit. You may find yourself saying, "The reason I hurt you was because you spoke harshly to me" or "The reason I'm so angry is because you hurt me."

My husband is so quick to repent that sometimes I get frustrated. When he realizes that he said something that hurt my feelings, he will say, "Oh honey, I'm so sorry. I was wrong to say that; please forgive me." Meanwhile I'm thinking, "No! I want to be angry for just a little bit longer because you hurt me." God says, "Be angry but do not sin" (Eph. 4:26, *RSV*). The religious spirit tries to get us to be angry and then to go on and sin by not forgiving as we should.

The spirit of religion is judgmental. Judging is another indication of religious pride. Do you find yourself looking around during church and thinking, *I wish they wouldn't sing this emotional song* or *People need to sit down* or *This dancing during worship is distracting* or something like that? The spirit of religion strives to get you to put yourself above others so that you will believe that you are holier or more spiritual than they.

When you find yourself criticizing someone else's actions or responses or motives, you may be under the influence of the religious spirit. This is the same spirit that operated in the Pharisees when they questioned Jesus for healing on the Sabbath. They wrongly judged His heart, motive and actions (see Matt. 12:10-13).

No Room for Grace

Under the influence of the religious spirit, the Pharisees judged others by the law. There was no room for grace or for mistakes. The same was true in my family as I grew up. As a military family, we lived under a lot of rules; and if we broke one—accidentally or on purpose—there was a penalty to pay. But God does not treat us that way. What a blessing it is to discover that God is bigger than any of our sins or mistakes, that Jesus paid every penalty and that grace abounds!

Some people believe that they have sinned so greatly that God cannot possibly forgive them for their sin. Divorcees, women who have had abortions and people who have committed sexual sins often live with tremendous guilt and shame. They may believe that God can forgive them, but they cannot forgive themselves. They do not allow grace to operate in their lives in order to become free, because the religious spirit fills their minds with lies like *You are too shameful to be forgiven* or *You are too shameful to be used by God.* It keeps reminding them of their mistakes, and it will not let them experience God's grace. If you have not received God's forgiveness for a sin in your life, then the religious spirit may well be holding you back.

Corrie ten Boom is known to have said, "It's a poor soldier indeed who does not recognize the enemy." Become one of God's skilled soldiers who can identify this spirit's tactics, including how it might affect you. After you grasp this and understand how your enemy strives to hold you back, you then can dismantle its plan of attack.

HOW THE RELIGIOUS SPIRIT ATTACKS

Two forms of attack that the spirit of religion uses in order to accomplish its plan to hold you back are bringing death and stealing from you. Let me explain.

Bringing Death

Bringing death is one of the main forms of attack that the religious spirit uses. Why? It hates Jesus—the way, the truth and the life (see John 14:6).

The spirit of religion will attempt to bring death to your hopes, your dreams, your vision and your call. This happens when you get to the point when you say, "I don't know if it even matters that I am here. Do I make a difference?" You do make a difference. God has a call for every one of us. He has a purpose, plan and destiny for your life. His desire is for you to fulfill your destiny. He will not confuse you when you get to a crossroads in your life and you need to know which way to go. He is standing there saying, "This is the way, walk in it" (Isa. 30:21).

In addition, the religious spirit will endeavor to bring death to relationships. It causes you to close your heart and to keep you from reconciling. It will drive you to seek revenge or retalia-tion. Some Christians get in arguments with others and then refuse to speak to them again.

Choose to walk in a lifestyle of forgiveness. If you do, you nullify the religious spirit's opportunity to bring death to rela-tionships. Be quick to repent, quick to forgive and quick to rec-oncile. Keep the enemy from getting a foothold in your soul. Give up the right to retaliate or hold a grudge. Extend grace to others and to yourself as well.

Stealing from You

Another form of attack that the religious spirit often uses is stealing. Jesus said, "The thief comes only to steal and kill and destroy; I have come that they may have life, and have it to the full" (John 10:10, *NIV*).

The religious spirit purposes to steal your joy. In doing so, it actually steals your strength (see Neh. 8:10). Once your joy is taken from you, your strength is also taken. When your strength is stolen, it becomes more difficult to resist demonic attacks.

As your joy is stolen, your faith is also diminished. If you don't see a word or a promise for you come to fruition, you can find yourself thinking, *Why should I believe this anymore? It's just too hard.* The religious spirit attempts to discourage you—to keep you from agreeing with what God says about you.

Maintain your joy and build your faith by speaking God's promises. As you do this, your faith increases (see Rom. 10:17). As your faith increases, so do your joy and your strength.

HOW TO PROTECT YOUR SOUL

Jesus set a precedent for successfully protecting our souls from the attacks of the religious spirit. In Luke 4, verses 4, 8 and 12,

Jesus directly confronted Satan by boldly declaring the truth of the Word. He countered every attack with confidence in God's character and His Word. As a result, Satan departed from Him.

You, too, can resist the religious spirit with the powerful weapon of the Word. Learn from Jesus. Tune your will to God's will and declare the truth of God's Word over your life. Remind your enemy of its defeat by saying what God says: "[The devil] will flee from you" (Jas. 4:7).

Put God First

The war in the heavens is over who will be worshipped. One way Satan receives worship is when the religious spirit operates in your life. This is done when you put people, situations, agendas, things or yourself above God. The first commandment says, "You shall have no other gods before Me" (Exod. 20:3). Open your mouth and declare to the heavenly hosts that you will serve no other gods and that you will have no other master but Jesus. Protect your soul by deciding to put God first in every area of your life.

The religious spirit subtly convinces you that other things are more important than being where God has called you to be, and it hinders you from being in the right place at the right time. You may erroneously believe that you don't need to be at church for the worship time, but only for the pastor's sermon. Deciding that worship isn't important indicates that your relationship with God isn't important. Worship prepares your heart for God to speak to you through the message.

While you are in God's presence, He stokes the flame of love that burns within you. Passion rises from intimate worship. Shield your soul from the religious spirit by capturing moments of worship to the most high God. When God is first in your life, you can't help but be passionate.

God's desire is for you to be passionate (see Rom. 12:10-11), while at the same time the religious spirit strives to steal your passion. It attempts to quench the fire of the Holy Spirit by getting you to cover up or diminish your love for the Lord. Moses had the same problem. His face glowed after being in God's presence. The children of Israel were afraid to come close to him, so he put a veil over his face (see Exod. 34:29-35).

> **Don't sit in your rocking chair and let the world pass you by. Choose to leave this life in a blaze of glory, filled with passion.**

When your passion is stirred up, people may respond like Moses' followers: "Why are you so intense? What happened to you? Put a lid on it." Your passion will make others uncomfortable, but do not yield. If the enemy can steal your passion, then he will be able to steal the revival that God is bringing into your life.

When passion begins to wane, you start believing that God doesn't need or want to use you anymore. As people grow older, they often think, *Well, I've done everything, so I might as well kick back and relax.* Don't buy into this lie; be zealous and passionate. Choose to leave this life in a blaze of glory, filled with passion. Don't sit in your rocking chair and let the world pass you by.

Die Daily

In order to put God first, you must make it a practice to die daily. Wake up every morning and have a funeral—yours! Paul set the example for us (see 1 Cor. 15:31). Choose to die to your flesh, your hopes, your plans, your emotions, your ways, your agenda—the list goes on. Die to all of you, but don't stay dead. Allow God to raise you with new life in Christ. Choose His ways, His plans, His agenda, His will, His desires and His purposes. Choose all of God and none of you.

Guard your soul from the religious spirit by choosing to die daily. When you have a really bad day, stop your grumbling and complaining. Remember, it's your flesh, your old sin nature, that is rising up again. Move out of your flesh and walk in the Spirit. Choose to die one more time and keep moving into your destiny.

Get Dressed

Take time to put on your spiritual clothing. The spirit of religion prefers you to wear garments of bitterness, anger, pity, hatred, unforgiveness, disunity and more. But God, the Designer, has made designer clothing for you to wear instead. Each piece represents what He wants to do in and through you. Protect your soul from the religious spirit by putting on this designer wardrobe:

- The Lord Jesus Christ (see Rom. 13:14)
- A new self (see Col. 3:10)
- A garment of praise (see Isa. 61:3)
- Compassion, kindness, humility, gentleness, patience and love (see Col. 3:12,14)
- Faith, love and the hope of salvation (see 1 Thess. 5:8)
- The armor of light (see Rom. 13:12)
- The full armor of God (see Eph. 6:13-17)

Walk in Truth

Some time ago I was praying in church with a woman who said,

"God spoke to me and told me I am to leave my husband and children and go to the mission field. I am to have no contact with them." I quickly replied, "That was *not* the voice of God. He does *not* speak that way!" The religious spirit had twisted the truth just enough that it sounded spiritual for her to go to the mission field and leave everyone behind.

The spirit of religion quotes the Word of God out of context. Though it knows what the truth is, it uses this truth to deceive and bring death. It is better to live in the tree of the life rather than in the tree of the knowledge of good and evil (see Gen. 2:9). This way you avoid using the Word of God to wound people or to make a point. You need to know God's Word, His heart and His character. Ask yourself, "What would God say?" Then say what He would say and do what He tells you to do. Remember, God will not tell you to do something contrary to His Word.

The religious spirit may convince you that God doesn't speak to you anymore—or that He has never spoken to you. Are you a child of God? If so, Jesus said, "My sheep hear My voice, and I know them" (John 10:27). You *can* hear God's voice.

As the religious spirit attacks your mind, choose to "[take] every thought captive to the obedience of Christ" (2 Cor. 10:5, *NASB*). You have the mind of Christ, so begin to think as God designed you to think (see 1 Cor. 2:16). Set your faith to believe that the Word of God has transforming power, and renew your mind (see Rom. 12:2). Guard your soul by setting your will to seek truth, believe truth, walk in truth and speak truth. These actions will silence the voice of the enemy in your mind.

Walk in Your Authority

God has not just given you authority; He has given you *His* authority. But the religious spirit can cause you to abdicate your authority. When you relinquish your position of authority, you open the door for the enemy to come in and attack you and your family. You are not some weak, wimpy person whom God put on the earth. God says you will possess the gates of your enemies (see Gen. 22:17). Purpose to take back what you have relinquished, what you gave up to the enemy. Rise up and be part of the mighty army that God has called, destined and ordained for you to be part of. Shield your soul by wearing the mantle He has given you and by walking with confidence in your authority.

Walk in the Fullness of the Spirit

Finally, walk in the fullness of the Holy Spirit. Honor God more than you honor people or tradition. Fear God more than you fear people, and you will no longer be performance oriented, no longer a people pleaser, no longer caring about what others think. Resist the enemy. Take time to sit before the Lord. Communicate with Him. Find out who God really is, what He thinks and what He says. Choose to apply these truths to your life every day. Discover your gifts and then embrace them into your life. As you continue to put these steps into practice, you'll become free from the religious spirit and able to stay free.

So get free from the religious spirit today and stay free! You will be changed and others will be blessed. Fulfill your destiny!

Chapter Seven

THE FRUIT OF "RELIGION"

KIMBERLY DANIELS

Dr. Kimberly Daniels is the apostle and overseer of Spoken Word Ministries in Jacksonville, Florida. She and her husband, Ardell, share a vision, based on Luke 11:33, of teaching, training and activating spiritual principles into the lives of Christians. A graduate of Florida State University and Jacksonville Theological Seminary, Kim holds degrees ranging from an associate through a doctorate in secular and biblical education.

An apostolic pioneer, Kimberly has ministered in England, Germany, Asia and throughout the world. Ordained under Apostle John Eckhardt's Crusaders Ministries in Chicago, Illinois, her athletic ability and military background help equip her in releasing warfare strategies to the Body of Christ.

She is the author of Against All Odds, From a Mess to a Miracle *and* Clean House—Strong House. *Her CD productions include* Demonbustin' Praise *and* Devil, Boo I See You. *Kim has been highlighted on ABC,* The 700 Club, Trinity Broadcasting Network, Daystar Television Network, *and in* Florida Times Union, Charisma *and* Ministries Today. *She is the proud mother of six children.*

The terms "spirit of religion" and "religious spirit" are commonly spoken from church pulpits today. The operation of the religious spirit cannot be categorized by a person's denomination, race or the way that person dances or is dressed in a church service. The truth is that the religious spirit operates in virtually every setting where the gospel is preached. It is a spirit that is assigned to distract people from the truth by making them think that where they are is okay.

GENUINE RELIGION OR RELIGIOSITY?

As believers, if we are not watchful, we can easily slip into religiosity. Religiosity can be any form of repetition. I often joke that I used to "religiously" go to the crack house. I thank God for making me sensitive to the bondage of addiction. I needed a radical change. Some people only go to church because they are religiously addicted. They also need a radical change.

In some groups "religion" has even become a bad word. biblically speaking, however, there is such a thing as genuine religion. James wrote,

If any man among you seem to be religious, and bridleth not his tongue, but deceiveth his own heart, this man's religion is in vain. Pure religion and undefiled before God and the Father is this, To visit the fatherless and widows in their affliction, and to keep himself unspotted from the world (Jas. 1:26-27, *KJV*).

This word "pure," in James 1:26, is *katharos* in Greek, and it also means "clean" and "clear."[1] Something that is pure is clean inside and out. The problem with the spirit of religion is that it only focuses on the outside of a person; the inside remains the same. Second Timothy 3:1-5 (*KJV*) describes what I am talking about perfectly. These verses read,

> This know also, that in the last days perilous times shall come. For men shall be lovers of their own selves, covetous, boasters, proud, blasphemers, disobedient to parents, unthankful, unholy, without natural affection, trucebreakers, false accusers, incontinent, fierce, despisers of those that are good, traitors, heady, high-minded, lovers of pleasures more than lovers of God; having a form of godliness, but denying the power thereof: from such turn away.

TELLTALE FRUIT

The Bible says that we can recognize a tree by the fruit that it bears (see Matt. 12:33-37). So 2 Timothy 3:1-5 can help us understand how to recognize the religious spirit. This passage lists what I believe to be 19 manifestations of the religious spirit in the lives of people in the Church. It would be easy to think that these manifestations occur in people who do not profess to be followers of Christ, but I personally take the position that these manifestations occur in people within the Church. One reason is because these people are described as "having a form of godliness" (v. 5). People who are influenced by the religious spirit preach the gospel, but they do not live it. And they deny the true power of God, rendering their religion powerless.

WITCHCRAFT IN RELIGION

I believe that the spirit of religion is responsible for taking millions of people to hell. According to Isaiah, God's people were destroyed (sent into captivity) because they had "no knowledge" (Isa. 5:13). They were deceived into believing they could count on gods and spirits other than the true God. Later, this passage goes on to say, "Hell hath enlarged herself, and opened her mouth without measure" (v. 14, *KJV*).

There are many warnings in the Bible against the spirit of religion. I find it very interesting that 2 Timothy 3:1-7 speaks of people who are under the influence of the religious spirit and that the next verse touches on witchcraft. This verse of Scripture talks about Jannes and Jambres, two magicians in the court of Pharaoh (according to Jewish tradition) who attempted to compare their power to the power of God (see Exod. 7:11). In the New Testament, there are continual warnings against false teachers and false religion (see 2 Cor. 11:13,26; Gal. 2:4; Phil. 3:2). The Bible recognizes that purveyors of false religion may appear religious and may even accomplish miracles. But if they lead people away from the one true God, they are to be shunned (see Deut. 18:9-17).

In Galatians 5:19-20, witchcraft is listed as one of the "works of the flesh" (*KJV*) or "acts of the sinful nature" (*NIV*). In the New Testament, the words "witchcraft" and "sorcery" come from the Greek word *pharmakeia,* and can include the administering of drugs, poisoning or practicing magical arts.[2] Witchcraft is an attempt to contact, control or manipulate supernatural beings or powers, or the spirits of the dead, through various incantations, spells and occult practices. It can appear as innocent spiritual forms and practices, or it can appear as dark and anti-God. Either way, the spirit of religion seeks to keep people from the knowledge of Jesus and the gospel.

MAGIC CAN WORK

Let me give you an example. Recently a young lady came to our midweek service. I noticed that her hair was falling out of her head from the roots. We prayed for her sister, and then we invited her to the altar also. Sarcastically, she told me that she did not need prayer. She also told me that I needed to go to her church with her. When she mentioned the name of her church, my prayer team alerted me that it was a local cult. This group sells numbers for gambling and has a $25 prayer line for private prophecies, but they call their organization a church. The foundation of their ministry approach is through religious repetition. For example, they may tell a person to drink a glass of water out of a cup for seven days for a financial blessing. Another popular scheme is to wear a T-shirt backward for a week to a courtroom in order to be given a lesser sentence. The scary part of all this is that people are getting results. The people would not continue to go back if it did not appear to be working.

Things like this may work but they are demonically orchestrated. Ecclesiastes 10:8 teaches that if a hedge is broken, a serpent will bite. There is a thin line between darkness and light. (Our spiritual discernment must be sharp enough not to cross the perimeters of God. The Hebrew word for "bite" can also be translated as "to oppress with interest on a loan."[3] People may get their temporary fixes through the dark side, but there is a high interest rate in the end. False ministers using the power of the spirit of religion give people accurate prophecies and formulas for every problem they have, but the end of it all is death.

The young lady in my midweek service began to brag about her religious leaders and how they could predict things in her life. She bragged that her boyfriend's court case was dropped after these leaders had prophesied. They also told her that her boyfriend would never leave her if she read a certain psalm every day and took spiritual baths. The Holy Spirit led me to minister to her prophetically. I told her that God showed me that she was prostituting for her boyfriend and that he had beaten her many times. I prophesied that God did not want him in her life because he was a womanizer and cared nothing about her. She broke down into tears, and my team began to minister deliverance to her. We broke the religious witchcraft off of her life!

THE SERIOUSNESS OF DEMONIC STRONGHOLDS

Why am I focusing on a case like this that many believers will never consciously experience? It is simple: Because in the eyes of God, all strongholds of religious form—from legalism to religious cults—are serious. The example of Hymenaeus and Philetus illustrate the seriousness with which God views strongholds. Though Hymenaeus and Philetus were in the Church, their words became like cancer when they erred concerning the truth (see 2 Tim. 2:17-18). These two men were religious leaders in the Church, but, just like Jannes and Jambres, they were on their way to hell. First Timothy 1:20 says that Hymenaeus and Alexander were delivered to Satan so that they would learn not to blaspheme.

When it comes to recognizing witchcraft, many believers do not have a clue. As a result, religious forms of witchcraft operate undetected in the house of the Lord. Whether the witchcraft reveals itself in the controlling spirit of an insecure leader or in the sorcery of a magician in a black cape, it is all the same in the eyes of God.

In the Bible, the difference between a true act of God and its counterfeit was clear. For example, the power of God was demonstrated as being superior to that of the Egyptians when Moses' snake swallowed the snakes of Pharaoh's magicians (see Exod. 7:10-12). And in 1 Kings 18:20-40, Elijah put the prophets of Baal to open shame in order that the people could see the difference between God and Baal and decide whom they would follow. Many in the Church have never been taught the difference between witchcraft and the works of God because witchcraft is seldom challenged in the house of the Lord. The result is that people can end up seeing the things of the devil and saying, "Thank You, Jesus!" simply because what they see is religious.

THE DECEPTION OF RELIGIOUS FORMS

Ephesians 3:20 says that with the same measure of power that works in us, God does great things. Religion denies this power to individual believers, leaving them bound by forms. A generation of people who are bound by forms will eventually become a generation who run after signs. Such a generation Jesus called "evil and adulterous" (Matt. 12:39). He also referred to these people as hypocrites and said that they could not "discern the signs of the times" (Matt. 16:3). People who have a form of godliness and no depth or power on the inside of them will be addicted to religious signs and will open themselves to deception.

Because of this, some people allow themselves to be led around by people whose ministry gifts only have a form of godliness. This word "form" is *morphosis* in Greek; it is a noun meaning "appearance."[4] "Morphosis" comes from the Greek verb *morphoo,* which means "to fashion."[5] There is a religious style in the

Church that can draw great crowds. People gather in massive numbers, but the curse is that they leave the meetings the same way that they came. They are stirred up in the fleshly realm only, never coming in contact with enough power to penetrate the strongholds of their personal lives.

The stronghold of religious forms can keep people from the true power of God.

The stronghold of religious forms can keep people from the true power of God. The spirit of religion wants believers to be satisfied with form alone. It produces counterfeit power, preventing believers from moving into the deeper things of God! While it is the simplicity of the Gospel that gets us saved, it is the deeper things of God that take us to our next level of maturity.

BEWARE OF THE DOGS!

In Philippians 3:2 Paul gives another serious warning: "Beware of dogs . . . !" The Greek word for "dog," *kuon,* may be translated either literally as "dog" or metaphorically as "a man of impure mind."[6] I may be stretching the point a bit, but I believe that this could refer to people who are under the influence of the religious spirit—religious hounds.

The first point I would like to bring out about this group of religious people whom Paul called "dogs" is that they were in no way in submission to the Master. Though they may have been religious and did things in His name, they were not truly led by Jesus. Jesus told the religious Pharisees that they were of their father, the devil (see John 8:44). So this means that there can be religious people in the Church who have been fathered by the devil.

We are in a time in the history of the Church when apostolic government is being restored. The religious spirit attempting to counteract the apostolic is apostasy. There is a line that is being drawn in the Spirit that will separate the wheat from the tares (see Matt. 13:24-30,36-43). God's people will be sharp to discern the difference between the "sent ones" of the apostolic and the "fallen away ones" of the apostasy. The ones who have actually fallen away and who frequently persist in hanging around the Church might possibly be the dogs that Paul referred to.

I would also like to suggest that there are those who purport to be Christian leaders but who, like stray dogs, wander around feeding on whatever they can find. They are religiously ambitious and are determined to achieve their goals by any means necessary. Whatever they have to do to get finances or to get fame, they will do! Paul warned the Church in biblical times, and I do the same today, to beware of the religious dogs! They are religious hounds that sniff out and prey on the weak or the spiritually ignorant in order to get whatever they can get out of them.

Furthermore, in the Bible, the word "dogs" can also refer to something that is unclean (see Matt. 7:6; Mark 7:27; Luke 16:21), which includes the religious spirit. The dogs that Paul referred to are people who are influenced by the religious spirit. They do not look evil. They do not associate with the occult or wear black capes and carry pitchforks. Rather, they look exactly like people who sincerely serve the Master.

A CLOSER LOOK AT THE FRUIT

There is a saying that one bad apple spoils the whole barrel. If bad fruit continues to hide out in the midst of good fruit, the whole barrel will be affected. In order to prevent bad fruit from causing good fruit to rot, the true nature of the bad fruit must be exposed, and the bad fruit must be separated out from the good fruit. Similarly, I believe that God is about to expose those in authority who have allowed themselves to be influenced by the spirit of religion and to lead them to repentance, or separate them from the life of the Church so that they cannot deceive others.

One aspect of the deception that these leaders have taught is participating in religious practices without involving one's heart. Prayer can be done using vain repetitions, which Jesus said is the way heathens pray (see Matt. 6:7). The Greek word for "vain repetitions" is *battologeo,* which literally means "to stutter" or "to prate tediously."[7] Immediately after Jesus warned against praying in this way, He gave the Lord's Prayer as our model for prayer (see vv. 9-13).

Unfortunately, the spirit of religion has succeeded in causing people to pray with vain repetitions when they pray the Lord's Prayer. (I used to pray it that way.) Jesus meant for the Lord's Prayer to be a guideline for prayer and not a memorized chant. Jesus said that though many people honor God with their mouth, their hearts are far from Him (see Matt. 16:8).

I would like to bring out two other points about fruit that relate to the fruit of "religion." First of all, fruit is the ripened ovary of a seed-bearing plant.[8] The continual reproduction of seed-bearing fruit is similar to that of the fruit of the spirit of religion. If the Church does not deal with this spirit's fruit, this fruit will continue to reproduce itself. The fruit that this spirit bears is empty things intended to lead people astray. In Jeremiah

10:3 the prophet talked about how the customs of the people were "vain" (*KJV*). The word "vain" is *hebel*, meaning "emptiness" and "unsatisfactory."[9] "Hebel" comes from another Hebrew word, *habal*, which means "to lead astray."[10] To protect the unity of the faith, which is one of Christ's goals for His Body (see Eph. 4:13), we must be watchful for the growth of this fruit that could potentially lead others astray.

Second, fruit is the edible part of the plant. The most dangerous thing about the fruit of the spirit of religion is that people tend to swallow it. The Bible tells us to taste and see that the Lord is good. God is so good that when we taste of His goodness, we always come out better. However, the taste of the fruit of the spirit of religion is bitter, and it makes those who eat it bitter, not better. When people eat this fruit, they end up empty and unsatisfied.

THE ARISING GENERATION

No matter how strong the grip of the spirit of religion on the Church appears to be, there is hope, for a new generation has arisen, one that will not swallow what this spirit has presented over the years. The people of this generation will walk in the anointing of the Father as they join themselves with this end-time move of the Holy Spirit. They will reject what God rejects, spitting anything out of their mouths that is not of His Spirit. Will you, too, choose to be part of this generation?

Chapter Eight

THE SPIRIT OF RELIGION IN THE LOCAL CHURCH

CHRIS HAYWARD

Chris Hayward is the president of Cleansing Stream Ministries, an organization dedicated to equipping local churches for biblically balanced, sound and effective deliverance ministry. Before his time with Cleansing Stream Ministries, Chris was the senior pastor at Christian Fellowship Church in Mount Vernon, Illinois. He currently makes his home in Castaic, California, with his wife, Karen. They have three children and two grandchildren.

The spirit of religion is the meanest, foulest, most ruthless spirit you will ever confront. (How's that for a beginning?) As an experienced pastor I can tell you this without equivocation.

HOW TO DESTROY A BRIDGE

From time to time I enjoy watching old war movies. On one particular evening, I became quite interested in the story line of one of these movies, *Force 10 from Navarone*. It is about a small group of commandos assigned to go behind enemy lines during World War II. These men joined with their allies to take out a bridge that their German enemies planned to use to bring their tanks across. The bridge had been unattainable because of the strong protection around it. One smart fellow, however, determined that if the dam upstream were to be blown up, it would result in a monumental flood that would in turn destroy the bridge. The commando unit fought its way into the dam as the explosives expert carefully set explosives in place. The explosives detonated as the soldiers raced up the surrounding hill to escape, killing a number of men.

To the dismay of the soldiers, the explosions seemed to have no effect. The dam stood in place. The commandos began to rail against the expert for setting the charges wrong. The expert calmly told them to watch. As they did, a rumble was heard, and then plaster began to fall away from the dam's facing. Before long, water began to seep out, and finally the dam gave way. The subsequent flood destroyed the bridge downstream.

CONFRONTATION WITH THE SPIRIT OF RELIGION

It was at this moment that the Lord spoke to my heart. He said, "When you speak the word I have given you for this Sunday, it will have the same effect as the floodwater, which destroyed the bridge." I thought, *Wow, that's great!* Little did I know what was about to transpire.

The Lord had given me a message about Ahab, Jezebel and the spirit of control. This spirit works in close conjunction with the religious spirit. In preparing for this word, I had no awareness of a problem in my church. To my way of thinking it was simply a preventative message. During the message, however, I kept wondering why certain people were staring at me as if they were angry. After that Sunday, I lost no fewer than 10 families, which at that time represented about 20 percent of our active members!

This was a very enlightening confrontation with the spirit of religion. At first I was downhearted, but I soon realized that it was for the best. God was faithful to His word, and after that

Pray—and then pray some more! Pray before you confront, pray while you confront, and pray after you confront.

purging, we were able to move forward as a body of believers in ways that would have been met with stiff opposition had this not taken place. Now, more than a decade later, I have had several other dealings with this spirit. None of them was pleasant. In fact, all of them were painful. Yet I have personally grown and matured through the process.

To have any success in dealing with the religious spirit, you must learn to confront it quickly. If you compromise and allow it to take root, you will grieve the Spirit of God and most likely subject yourself and others to much frustration and heartache. The longer you wait, the more entrenched the religious spirit becomes. As with Elijah and the prophets of Baal and Asherah, you may need to confront this spirit with an all-out demonstration of the power of God.

I suggest that once you have decided to confront this spirit, you join yourself in prayer with a trusted group of believers to call on the Lord. Ask Him to undergird you with His wisdom and strength. Proclaim the Word, employ the power of the Cross, and begin to take authority over every demonic scheme that has been assigned against you. Give praise and thanksgiving for the One who is in you and who is greater than anything that is coming against you. Pray—and then pray some more! Pray before you confront, pray while you confront, and pray after you confront.

THE NATURE OF THE SPIRIT OF RELIGION

During Jesus' earthly stay He encountered the spirit of religion head-on through the Pharisees. He had more than a few words to say about these men. It is from one of these exchanges that we'll extrapolate some truths about the nature of spirit that worked through them. Let's look at Jesus' words in Matthew 23.

"Do as I say, not as I do."

They say, and do not do (Matt. 23:3).

The religious spirit is very quick to use its victims to point out the failures and needs of others, while being totally blind to their own shortcomings. In fact, it often induces people to criticize others in areas that they themselves lack.

A man in leadership at my church once told me that, as a church, we were hearing far too much about the subject of grace. "What is needed," he said, "is a strong dose of personal discipline and hard work." Discipline and hard work are virtuous qualities, yet he was the most undisciplined man I knew. For most of his life, he did not have to work hard. By imposing an unrealistically high standard for others, it gave him the illusion of personal accomplishment.

"Let me hand you another brick."

> They bind heavy burdens, hard to bear, and lay them on men's shoulders; but they themselves will not move them with one of their fingers (Matt. 23:4).

Those with the religious spirit will tend not only to expect more from you than from themselves but also to fail to stoop to your level and help you out. Sometimes religious leaders fall prey to this by demanding that certain members of their congregation attend every meeting and every training session with no regard for their stressed-out families. Then they tell them to be sensitive to their spouse and/or children by spending the appropriate time together.

"Ain't I great!"

> All their works they do to be seen by men. They make their phylacteries broad and enlarge the borders of their garments (Matt. 23:5).

One of the first places that the spirit of religion shows up is among those who seek recognition. This usually happens in a very subtle way. Most all of us like and appreciate recognition. The question is, Do we need and require that recognition from others, or are we content to receive it from God in His way and in His time? Whether we seek recognition for the clothes we wear or the titles we seek, we are all vulnerable to the influence of this spirit. Once ensnared, a prideful heart can cause others to be fearful should they fail to acknowledge that person's position or value before others.

"Move over! That's my spot!"

> They love the best places at feasts, the best seats in the synagogues, greetings in the marketplaces, and to be called by men, "Rabbi, Rabbi" (Matt. 23:6-7).

Not only does the spirit of religion cause people to seek recognition for *what they do*, but it also causes people to seek approval for *who they are*. A number of years ago I experienced this first-hand, and the lesson I learned was forged deeply into my soul.

I used to serve as the assistant of the well-known writer and speaker Walter Martin. He would be asked to speak before huge assemblies, and he was deeply respected for his knowledge. While working with him, I had the privilege of spending a great deal of time with him.

One time we were at a well-known church. Martin was set to speak at this large gathering, but he first spent some time with the pastor in his study to pray. I proceeded to go down to the roped-off area designated for the speaker and other pastors. Since I assumed that everyone obviously should know of my importance, I simply removed the rope and sat down. I was aware of many eyes looking at me, wondering who this important fellow could be. Before long, I heard footsteps behind me approaching my location. An imposing looking deacon stood before me. He simply said, "Sir, you'll have to move now. These seats are reserved for the pastors." The same eyes that viewed me taking a seat now watched as I sheepishly got up and moved to the back. As I walked that ever-so-long walk up the aisle, I heard the words of the Lord saying, "If you are invited to a wedding feast, don't always head for the best seat. What if someone more respected than you has also been invited? The host will say, 'Let this person sit here instead.' Then you will be embarrassed and will have to take whatever seat is left at the foot of the table! Do this instead—sit at the foot of the table. Then when your host sees you, he will come and say, 'Friend, we have a better place than this for you!' Then you will be honored in front of all the other guests" (Luke 14:8-10, *NLT*).

It was only later that I realized that I had been victimized by the spirit of religion.

"We've never done it that way before, and we're not going to start now!"

> But woe to you, scribes and Pharisees, hypocrites! For you shut up the kingdom of heaven against men; for you neither go in yourselves, nor do you allow those who are entering to go in (Matt. 23:13).

Up to this point Jesus had described the inner character of those whose are under the influence of the religious spirit. Then He began to examine how this spirit manifests itself outwardly against others. The first four statements show just how prideful this spirit is. But now we begin to see its poisonous results. The Bible states, "Out of the abundance of the heart the mouth speaks" (Matt. 12:34). The abundance of pride now seeks to put a stop to anything or anyone who would dare suggest that something or someone other than itself should run the show. Herein is another key to identifying the religious spirit at work: It will always seek to stop the work of the Holy Spirit. And the reason is simple: *If the Holy Spirit is in charge, the spirit of religion is not!*

When the Holy Spirit is in charge, we still need great wisdom in initiating the new and innovative directions that He gives us.

When we head into new directions, we go against the status quo, so we need wisdom and courage as we go forward. Jesus brought about a break with tradition by relieving His disciples of the responsibility of fasting. When He was questioned about their failure to fast, Jesus responded by saying, "No one puts a piece of unshrunk cloth on an old garment; for the patch pulls away from the garment, and the tear is made worse. Nor do people put new wine into old wineskins, or else the wineskins break, the wine is spilled, and the wineskins are ruined. But they put new wine into new wineskins, and both are preserved" (Matt. 9:16-17). With those words Jesus offered sound advice on how to bring (and also how not to bring) the new into the old: The new must be carried in new wineskins.

I know of an evangelical church where the leadership wanted to embrace more of the Holy Spirit in the life of the church body. Matthew 9:16-17 became the leaders' model for bringing this change, and they sought for a wise and loving way to do so. Their church was quite traditional, and many of the members would not easily receive such a change. At the time, the church had a poorly attended midweek service. The leaders chose this service to be the new wineskin to allow the Holy Spirit to move with greater freedom. Rather than bringing this change into the main Sunday services and risk the possibility of tearing apart the church, the leadership instead wisely brought it to the midweek service. Over time the number of people who attended the midweek service grew larger than the number who attended the regular Sunday morning services. Those who participated on Wednesday began to spill in to the regular Sunday morning services. Through time and patience the pastor led this growing congregation and their newfound freedom in the Spirit to find a balanced and scriptural place within the life of the church body.

As I have already written, the religious spirit is dead-set

against the work of the Holy Spirit. Those who are under demonic influence will always oppose God's purposes. They will always seek to undermine any leader who attempts to bring the fresh wind of His presence into the Body of Christ. Many a battle has been lost at this juncture. The very breath of the Bride will be extinguished if the spirit of religion has its way.

Having said that, I need to make it clear that not all resistance to the initiatives of leadership is the result of the religious spirit. Sometimes impatience or lack of wisdom on the part of a leader can cause much unnecessary upheaval within church life. Prayer, patience and submission to the leading of the Holy Spirit are imperative both for the leaders who implement change and for those who confront the religious spirit.

In addition, we need to be aware that in our opposing what we believe to be the religious spirit, we might inadvertently be used by this spirit in our dealings with others. For example, we might actually find ourselves using control and manipulation against someone whom we feel is being used as a puppet by that very same spirit. In Matthew 7:3-5 we are warned of this danger:

> Why do you look at the speck in your brother's eye, but do not consider the plank in your own eye? Or how can you say to your brother, "Let me remove the speck out of your eye"; and look, a plank is in your own eye? Hypocrite! First remove the plank from your own eye, and then you will see clearly to remove the speck out of your brother's eye.

Once we Christian leaders discern how the spirit of religion is operating in a particular situation, we must confront it. Through much prayer and courageous action, we must pursue this spirit's defeat, no matter the cost. During World War II

France made the mistake of compromising with Hitler. France was almost immediately occupied, and the people lost their freedom. The same thing can happen in the local church, so we must not compromise with the spirit of religion. There can only be either liberty or bondage—and nothing in between.

"Come into my parlor," said the spider to the fly.

> Woe to you, scribes and Pharisees, hypocrites! For you devour widows' houses, and for a pretense make long prayers. Therefore you will receive greater condemnation (Matt. 23:14).

Taking advantage of the helpless condition of widows, the Pharisees, who excelled in being led by the spirit of religion, contrived unethical means to steal their homes and their livelihood, all this while uttering great and influential prayers. The spirit of religion is, at its heart, self-centered and greedy. It seeks its own welfare and will ride over anyone who gets in its way, while all the way sounding spiritual. Those under its influence will pervert God's will and twist His Word to achieve their own selfish goals.

I once walked in on a church meeting in which I saw the visiting minister holding up nails for the congregation to see. He said that these nails, which he had found on a recent trip to Jerusalem, "could be the actual nails from our dear Savior's cross." He suggested to the very elderly audience that they should bring forth their social security checks and endorse them to his ministry. He assured them that they would find greater security in "holding close to their heart" one of their Savior's nails. Several widows actually came forward! This made me detest the spirit of religion even more than I had before.

"Oh, that I were made judge in the land."

> Woe to you, scribes and Pharisees, hypocrites! For you travel land and sea to win one proselyte, and when he is won, you make him twice as much a son of hell as yourselves (Matt. 23:15).

We can see the characteristic that Jesus exposed here very clearly illustrated in 2 Samuel 15. David had initially turned against his son Absalom for avenging the death of Absalom's sister Tamar. In time Absalom was permitted back to the palace, but not before bitterness had set in to Absalom's heart. And in keeping with the nature of the religious spirit, he began to look for ways to draw attention to himself and eventually to take control, overthrowing his father.

Here is the story: "After this it happened that Absalom provided himself with chariots and horses, and fifty men to run before him. Now Absalom would rise early and stand beside the way to the gate. So it was, whenever anyone who had a lawsuit came to the king for a decision, that Absalom would call to him and say, 'What city are you from?' And he would say, 'Your servant is from such and such a tribe of Israel.' Then Absalom would say to him, 'Look, your case is good and right; but there is no deputy of the king to hear you.' Moreover Absalom would say, 'Oh, that I were made judge in the land, and everyone who has any suit or cause would come to me; then I would give him justice.' And so it was, whenever anyone came near him to bow down to him, that he would put out his hand and take him and kiss him. In this manner Absalom acted toward all Israel who came to the king for judgment. So Absalom stole the hearts of the men of Israel" (2 Sam. 15:1-6).

Absalom's actions that are narrated in 2 Samuel 15 are characteristic of people under the influence of the spirit of religion. The following are indicative of people who harbor this spirit:

1. They seek to gather those around them who will applaud their virtues and stand with them in their outlook (see v. 1).
2. They look for ways to gain the attention of others (see v. 2).
3. They look for ways to subvert divine order by having others report their complaints to them, rather than to God-given authority (see vv. 2-3).
4. They seek to demean and slander legitimate authority (see v. 3).
5. They infer that they would be a better leader if given the opportunity (see v. 4).
6. They feign humility, while all the while bloated with pride (see v. 5).
7. They eventually steal the hearts of the congregations of the local churches (see v. 6).

"Here, swallow another camel."

Woe to you, scribes and Pharisees, hypocrites! For you pay tithe of mint and anise and cummin, and have neglected the weightier matters of the law: justice and mercy and faith. These you ought to have done, without leaving the others undone. Blind guides, who strain out a gnat and swallow a camel! (Matt. 23:23-24).

Those who are influenced by the religious spirit have a way of majoring on the minors and minoring on the majors. Failing to see the bigger picture of advancing the kingdom of God, they prefer to argue over the color of the carpeting or to threaten mutiny should you dare have the audacity to move the organ over to the other side of the sanctuary. To them, tradition and image are everything. In their eyes, the poor are a disgrace to the community, and the wounded and hurting must have somehow come into disfavor with the Lord. They fail to perceive why anyone would want to go to, what they consider to be, a God-forsaken country, such as India or Somalia, when there are needs in their own backyard. They're proud of their tithe, and they expect an equal voice in how the church should be run. They are impatient with members in need, thinking that they should have been more careful with their finances.

"Hand me another rock to throw."

> Woe to you, scribes and Pharisees, hypocrites! Because you build the tombs of the prophets and adorn the monuments of the righteous, and say, "If we had lived in the days of our fathers, we would not have been partakers with them in the blood of the prophets." Therefore you are witnesses against yourselves that you are sons of those who murdered the prophets (Matt. 23:29-31).

Aside from seeking to quench the work of the Holy Spirit, the religious spirit also wants to kill off prophets. Prophets have an uncanny way of pointing out the truth. True prophets seek to do this without bringing undue focus on themselves, and they always want to build up the Body of Christ.

The prophetic voice is essential to a healthy growing church. It is a confirming gift that reaffirms God's Word and His direction. So I find it hard to understand why some people today reject the ministry of prophets—except to attribute it to the influence of the religious spirit. The religious spirit is unsettled when people rely on the Holy Spirit, because when they do, it threatens to expose this spirit's insidious nature and undermine its base of power and influence. In order to prevent this threat from becoming reality, the religious spirit seeks to undermine, discourage and destroy those who seek to speak words of life.

Many times I have seen Spirit-led disciples be severely attacked by those who have the spirit of religion. A young couple that joined the church that I pastored is one example. Both the husband and the wife gave their hearts to the Lord during a large evangelism service that came to the city. After meeting the Lord, they wanted only to serve Him with all their hearts. They shared their faith with everyone they could and were always ready to volunteer their time. This young couple's enthusiasm was a threat for one of our more seasoned saints, who had long since allowed himself to become hardened and bitter toward anyone more alive than he. As the pastor, I was required to intervene more than once to confront that spirit in this brother who once had been very much alive, and to encourage the young couple. Consistent with their hearts of love for the Lord, this couple made a point to pray for and bless the brother who had opposed them.

WHAT MUST WE DO?

Now that we know what the spirit of religion looks like and how it behaves in a local church situation, an important question remains: What are we to do about it? As I explained in the beginning of this chapter, the religious spirit is one of the most diabolical forces opposing the Body of Christ. It is bold, intimidating and ruthless. When it is present, it calls for a courageous leader to step forward.

The difficult nature of this spirit is that it hates to be revealed.

The people who are under its influence will go to great lengths to avoid any outward wrongdoing or weakness of character. When confronted, they attempt to make the confronters feel judgmental and divisive. As I stated before, if you allow this spirit room to operate and you fail to confront it, you will be in for a terrible time. As hard as it might be to deal with the spirit of religion, it must be done, or you will only face heartache down the road.

THE PRIORITY OF PRAYER

The first order of business is prayer. In the same manner that rain eventually softens dry, hardened dirt, so intense intercession will soften the hardened resistance of those who are in bondage to the religious spirit to confront the spirit. If their hearts fail to change, then the church leadership needs to do whatever is required to remove them from any position that could harm the congregation. The religious spirit will cause relationships to decay and will eventually bring about factions within the local church.

A THREE-STEP PROCESS TOWARD FREEDOM

However, let's assume that a fruitful confrontation has taken place, humility prevails, and those who recognize the influence of the religious spirit in them desire deliverance. What, then, is the process? In Cleansing Stream Ministries, we have found that all deliverance, including deliverance from the spirit of religion, requires three steps, which may be summed up with three words:

- Repent
- Renounce
- Break

We have found that, when dealing with the religious spirit, the repentance step will frequently involve repenting in areas of unforgiveness and participation in occult activity. Often, before coming to Christ, people are involved in the occult; and even uninformed believers may dabble in astrology, ouija boards or another activity associated with the occult.

Generational iniquity often needs to be repented of, renounced and broken as well. This includes those in their family line who gave in to the religious spirit. Because of their failure to repent and remove the legal ground that they gave to the spirit, that spirit tends to seek a victim within the same family bloodline with which to partner.

I have seen many cases in which individuals, who went by themselves before God with sincere and humble hearts, received deliverance. Others desire to submit themselves to church leadership and walk through the process of deliverance with them. While affirming the possibility of self-deliverance, I recommend involving the church leadership if at all possible.

I want to make this as simple of a process as I can. I have written a series of statements that can be used in deliverance. They can be read by individuals for self-deliverance or by church leadership, with the individuals repeating them.

Repent and Renounce

Generational

I repent and renounce every opening, known or unknown, that I have given to a religious spirit in my family line.

Personal Entry Points

I repent and renounce every opening, known or unknown, that I have given to a religious spirit, and every work or darkness connected with it.

Point 1: I repent for not fully receiving Your love, compassion, mercy, grace and forgiveness; and I renounce any belief that You, Lord, are distant and judgmental. I choose to embrace all aspects of Your character and to intimately know You.

Point 2: I repent for allowing myself to be led by any other spirit than the Holy Spirit.

I repent for relying on my own intellect in worship, praise, prayer, reading of the Word and spiritual warfare.

I repent and renounce all legalism, traditions and religious formulas.

I repent and renounce all participation in dead works.

I repent and renounce all dullness to the things of God.

I repent and renounce hardness of heart.

I choose for the oil of Your Holy Spirit to flow across my heart.

Point 3: I repent and renounce placing man's opinion of me above Yours.

I repent and renounce compromises: of the truth, of my integrity and of my purity.

I repent and renounce all compromises in my attitude toward sin.

I repent for my lack of transparency:

for covering sin,

for not confessing sin,

for not receiving correction,

for being defensive and quick to justify and rationalize my sin.

I repent and renounce all deception and hypocrisy.

I repent and renounce all pride, arrogance and self-righteousness.

I repent and renounce all comparison, judgment, criticism, gossip, jealousy, covetousness and anger.

I repent and renounce all persecution and slander of those moving in the Holy Spirit.

I repent and renounce every act of rebellion that has reinforced the spirit of religion in my life.

I choose to have obedience as my heart attitude.

I choose to no longer partner with the same spirit that killed Jesus and that continues to attempt to kill the work of the Holy Spirit today.

I choose to no longer oppose God.

Break

I break

every hex, curse or vow,

every spell, incantation or ritual.

I break

every covenant and blood covenant,

every sacrifice and blood sacrifice.

I break

every soul tie,

every generational tie in my family line.

I break any other legal right, known or unknown, for the spirit of religion to stay.

Spirit of religion, as the Body of Christ, I and those with me come against you:

We refuse to allow you to steal our intimate relationship with our Lord.

We refuse to allow you to kill the flow of the Holy

Spirit in us.

We refuse to allow you to destroy the anointing of others through us.

We choose to receive the anointing to break the power of the spirit of religion in the Church of Jesus Christ.

Once you and your congregation, with all sincerity, humility and submission to Christ, go through this list of statements and declarations, you can be assured that the religious spirit, no matter how deeply it has been imbedded, will leave. You will then be free to move powerfully into the destiny that God has for you and your church.

Chapter Nine

THE SPIRIT OF RELIGION, THE GREAT IMPOSTER

HANK AND MYRENE MORRIS

Hank and Myrene Morris are ordained pastors of the International Church of the Foursquare Gospel and are on the pastoral staff of The Church On The Way in Van Nuys, California, founded by Dr. Jack Hayford. They have been involved since the early 1970s in a wide variety of ministries, with an emphasis on discipling leaders. As the directors of Cleansing Stream Ministries at The Church On The Way, they teach extensively on the principles of spiritual warfare and deliverance. Their unique husband-and-wife team-teaching style makes them desired speakers for leadership conferences both in the United States and in other nations. Hank and Myrene's ministry is both Bible-based and practical.

They teach about everyday life in Jesus, including topics such as prayer, walking in the Spirit and intimacy with Jesus. They are also on the faculty of the Hayford Bible Institute, and Myrene is a frequent women's conference speaker. Hank and Myrene have been married since 1967 and have three children and two grandchildren.

To all of us who have received Jesus as Savior, there has come an expression of the sweeping grandeur of God's love. He has sent the Holy Spirit to live within us and empower us to fulfill the wonderful plan that God has for our lives.

OUR SPIRITUAL IMMUNE SYSTEM

Just as our bodies have a physical immune system to combat disease, so our spirits have an immune system to combat spiritual disease. And just as some diseases attack and destroy the body's immune system so that it has nothing to fight with, so our adversary, Satan, attacks us for the purpose of cutting us off from our spiritual immune system. This spiritual immune system is the strength and life we have in Christ under the direction and empowerment of the Holy Spirit. But Satan sends the spirit of religion to attack our spiritual immune system, causing us to live lives devoid of the presence and power of God. The spirit of religion is Satan's secret weapon.

OUR ADVERSARY'S SECRET WEAPON

The Bible refers to certain spirits by name: for example, a spirit of infirmity, a spirit named Legion, and a deaf and dumb spirit (see Luke 13:11; Mark 5:9; 9:25). But it does not refer to all by name. The Bible was not intended to be a textbook of demonology. It was intended to reveal God's character, the plan of salvation and the pathway to holiness and abundant life in Christ. However, since God does not intend for us to be ignorant of the devil's strategies to hold God's people in bondage (see Eph. 6:11), the Bible gives us much information about the demonic realm.

The spirit of religion, or the religious spirit, is one of those spirits that are not mentioned by name in the Bible, but it was nonetheless present and working in the events that are described there. This spirit deceived people and trapped them into "having a form of godliness but denying its power" (2 Tim. 3:5). And it animated the murderous ire and wrath of the scribes and Pharisees against Jesus. In turn, these scribes and Pharisees were the objects of Jesus' greatest wrath and condemnation. He called them hypocrites who, like whitewashed tombs, "appear beautiful outwardly, but inside are full of dead men's bones and all uncleanness" (Matt. 23:27). These were the men who directed the religious life of the people, but they did not live what they taught, and they rejected truth. The religious spirit knows that if spiritual leaders can be corrupted, those under them will also be corrupted. Leaders are its priority target.

Although the spirit of religion is an ancient spirit, it continues moving through the world with a vengeance today. In the process of destroying churches, as well as multitudes of individuals around the world, it masquerades as "true spirituality," and in that way becomes the great imposter. Those who are under its control are deceived into believing that their actions are religiously correct, thus blinding their minds to the suggestion that they might not be following God's order.

OUR SURE HOPE OF FREEDOM

The apostle Paul testified of himself that in former times

"according to the strictest sect of our religion I lived a Pharisee" (Acts 26:5). But as a result of his encounter with the Lord, Paul was delivered from the religious spirit, and he became a model of one who walks in the greatest sensitivity to the leading of the Holy Spirit. In fact, he became such a yielded vessel that he wrote 13 of the books of the New Testament. We believe that this is one of God's ways of telling us that *we can also be gloriously freed* from the religious spirit.

Freedom from the religious spirit is possible because God's power is infinitely greater than Satan's.

Freedom is possible because God's power is infinitely greater than Satan's, and God has given us authority to use that power so that we can be victorious over Satan. We receive power from the Holy Spirit, who is in us (see Acts 1:8). This is the same Holy Spirit by whom Jesus cast out demons (see Matt. 12:28). James 4:7 reads, "Resist the devil and he will flee from you"; and John declared, "He who is in you is greater than he who is in the world" (1 John 4:4). Believers have authority to cast out demons in the name of Jesus (see Mark 16:17), and we have the authority to bind our adversary and plunder his resources (see Matt. 12:29). Finally, "the weapons of our warfare are not carnal but mighty in God" (2 Cor. 10:4).

Before we discuss how we can use our authority to defeat the spirit of religion, we will detail how this adversary operates.

THE LIES AND DECEPTION OF OUR ADVERSARY

Lies and deception are the hallmark of the spirit of religion. Its target is the Body of Christ, both collectively and individually. Its ultimate purpose is to stop the move of God and the work of the Holy Spirit by cutting the Body off from the life and truth of God and from His Spirit. To do so, it fosters "religious" responses to problems and situations, responses that are devoid of the direction and power of the Holy Spirit. If we, the Body of Christ, succumb, we cannot be in a position to partner with God in His work. But this spirit is subtle enough to render us unaware of what is happening, deceiving us into believing that God is directing what we do when in fact He is not. It comes as an imposter masquerading as the real thing.

How does the religious spirit succeed in cutting believers off from relationship with God and blocking the work of the Holy Spirit?

1. *It cuts believers off from receiving God's love.* The religious spirit works to prevent us from receiving God's love, thereby preventing us from truly loving Him or loving others. In doing this, it blocks revelation of the most fundamental understanding in life, namely that God loves us.

2. *It stops believers from knowing God and being in His presence.* When we know God and are in His presence, God's reality is so intense that all other considerations fade into the shadows; and our resolve to serve Him, trust Him, bond with Him and depend on Him is strong. The religious spirit hates this and strives to block it.

3. *It strips believers of the direction and power of the Holy Spirit by keeping us in the flesh.* Many passages in God's Word describe the power and the work of the Holy

Spirit. Jesus said to His disciples before His ascension, "But you shall receive power when the Holy Spirit has come upon you" (Acts 1:8). If the religious spirit can get us to handle matters exclusively by our own resources, we will not see signs and wonders and other works of the Holy Spirit.

4. *It cuts off the flow of God's truth.* Without the truth of God flooding our being, we are prey to the deception and lies of the adversary. Jesus told those who believed in Him, "You shall know the truth, and the truth shall make you free"; but of Satan He said, "He is a liar and the father of it" (John 8:32,44). The religious spirit tries to enslave us with lies.

5. *It blocks believers from receiving God's forgiveness so that they continue in guilt and shame.* In 1 John 1:9 God promises that if we confess our sins, He will forgive us and cleanse us from all unrighteousness. Satan wants to keep us in torment and misery, so he constantly accuses us of sin and tells us the lie that our sins cannot be forgiven. That is why some Christians repeatedly ask for God's forgiveness for a particular sinful act they have committed. The religious spirit forbids them the joy of accepting the work of the Cross.

STRATEGIES OF THE SPIRIT OF RELIGION

How does the spirit of religion accomplish its goals? The Bible's descriptions of the Pharisees show what the religious spirit looks like in people who are under its influence. Furthermore, after having often dealt with individuals under the influence of the religious spirit, we have seen three major strategies that it frequently employs: (1) It opposes the entry of spiritual vitality and fresh revelation in believers; (2) it causes believers to focus on self and on carnal things rather than on the Holy Spirit; and (3) it fosters ideas and attitudes that separate believers from God and weaken their relationship with Him.

Let's look at these strategies one at a time.

Opposing the Entry of Spiritual Vitality and Fresh Revelation

Using a variety of methods, the religious spirit will oppose spiritual vitality and fresh revelation from entering followers of Christ. A number of these methods are as follows:

- *The religious spirit will move believers to depend on reasoning and intellect rather than on the guidance, power and revelation of the Spirit.* God's Word says, "Trust in the LORD with all your heart, and lean not on your own understanding" (Prov. 3:5). For example, if I have three conflicting commitments on the same evening—a church leadership meeting, a friend's birthday and my child's school function—I might reason that I cannot skip the church meeting, my spouse could cover the school meeting, and I could attend the friend's party at the end of the evening. If, however, I am moving in the Holy Spirit, I will inquire of the Lord rather than depend on my reasoning. He is all-knowing and He might well lead me to a different course of action.

- *The religious spirit pushes believers into legalism.* Legalism is defined as strict, literal or excessive conformity to a moral code. But the Word says, "The letter kills, but the Spirit gives life" (2 Cor. 3:6). If legalism sets in, we find ourselves fervently doing a "religious" work without the presence of the Holy Spirit.

  Some years ago I, Myrene, felt led of the Lord to

read six chapters of the Bible each day. I was diligently meeting my quota and was pleased with myself because I knew that reading God's Word is a vital part of a Christian's life. After a while though, I noticed that my focus shifted to finishing that day's requirement so that I could move on to whatever was next on my agenda. Worse than that, I realized that I was reading the Word without owning it. I was skimming over God's truth without letting it be absorbed. Finally, God, in His graciousness, showed me that a religious spirit had been robbing me by prompting me to read the Bible as a routine. When I rebuked that spirit, God gave me freedom, and Scripture reading became alive. The goal was no longer just quantity, but quality. The Scriptures became so thrilling that I often read six chapters or more; but more important, He began to change me through His Word in a way that couldn't have happened while that spirit was there.

• *The religious spirit influences believers to engage in and pursue matters of faith through formulas, rituals and traditional acts.* Our flesh likes the ease of copying, rather than seeking, the Holy Spirit's input and anointing. We sometimes find it easier to replicate what seems to be effective—another's phraseology, style or gestures—rather than seeking the Lord as to how He would have *us* proceed. Whether we are asking God to bless our food, saying "God bless you" when someone sneezes or laying hands on and praying for someone, everything must be done in partnership with the Holy Spirit. His fresh touch brings life. He will also help us to protect our worship. God desires that from our hearts we express our love to Him, instead of performing a perfunctory duty. When you sense that a religious spirit is trying to influence your worship, oppose it and ask the Holy Spirit to give you a spirit of praise.

- *The religious spirit causes people to pervert and twist the truth.* First Timothy 4:1 reads, "Some will depart from the faith, giving heed to deceiving spirits and doctrines of demons." The religious spirit does not want the truth of God to be declared, so it will cause a perversion of the truth to be presented as the real thing. At first glance, Satan's quotes of Scripture in Luke 4:1-13 sound convincing, but Jesus exposed Satan's distorted use of them.

- *The religious spirit blinds people to the truth.* The legalistic Pharisees opposed Jesus, who is the truth (see John 14:6). Jesus called the Pharisees "blind guides" (Matt. 23:24). This spirit particularly blinds people to the truth about the work of the Holy Spirit.

- *The religious spirit will make people unteachable.* James 1:22 instructs believers to "be doers of the word, and not hearers only, deceiving yourselves." But those who are deceived by the religious spirit, though they hear the truth, will not do it. As a couple, we frequently and fervently pray, "Dear God, help us to be teachable. Continue to change us." As long as the Holy Spirit has the freedom to work in our lives, we will be changing more and more into the image of Christ.

- *The religious spirit will induce believers to read God's Word only with their minds, without involving their hearts and spirits and without inquiring of the Holy Spirit.* When we read God's Word, the assistance of the Holy Spirit is vitally important because "no one knows the things of God except the Spirit of God" (1 Cor. 2:11). The Holy Spirit reveals what God wants to say to us through His Word. If our minds wander during Scripture reading and our hearts feel untouched by the Word, we should stop and pray, "Forgive me, Lord, for not reading Your Word in the Spirit. Religious spirit, I break your power over me in Jesus' name. Holy Spirit, help me read the Word under Your anointing so that I might be changed as the Word enters my heart."

- *The religious spirit will press believers to pray with their minds, rather than by the moving of the Spirit.* The Word says we are to be "praying always with all prayer and supplication in the Spirit" (Eph. 6:18). When we pray in the flesh, we can be concerned about the form or structure of the prayer, rather than following the Holy Spirit. Such prayers are stiff and lifeless.

- *A person under the influence of the religious spirit will persecute and slander those who move in the Spirit.* The Pharisees persecuted Jesus; those who are influenced by the religious spirit today will do the same.

- *The religious spirit will cause people to be hypocritical.* Hypocritical people teach the truth but do not do it; they are outwardly pious but inwardly corrupt. Jesus indicted the Pharisees for being hypocrites (see Matt. 23:25).

- *The religious spirit will cause people to be unable to discern the work or move of the Spirit.* The Pharisees thought that Jesus cast out demons by Beelzebub, the ruler of demons, instead of by the Holy Spirit (see Matt. 12:24).

Focusing on Self and on Carnal Things

Another strategy of the spirit of religion is to entice its victims to focus on themselves and on carnal things, rather than spiritual, things. The following are some examples of this strategy:

- *The religious spirit will cause believers to worship and pray with carnal motives.* This spirit will entice us to focus on ourselves rather than on God, to worry about whether we are "doing it right" and to want to impress others by how good we sound. Jesus accused the Pharisees of praying ostentatiously, to be seen by the crowd (see Matt. 6:5). Instead, we need to be focusing on God and submitting to the direction of the Holy Spirit.
- *The religious spirit will cause people to engage in dead works* (see Heb. 6:1). Dead works are, among other things, works of ministry implemented for soulish reasons. Of the Pharisees, Jesus said, "All their works they do to be seen by men" (Matt. 23:5). Some examples of soulish motives are a desire for praise or recognition, a desire to please certain people and a desire for the advancement of personal gain or interest. But when the work is by the Spirit, He initiates it, He anoints us for it, and the work is fulfilling and brings life and fruit that remain. When we are working with the Holy Spirit, we will be like a toaster making toast, doing exactly what we are designed to do.
- *The religious spirit entices believers to be judgmental of others and unforgiving of their failures.* The religious spirit will lead us to compare ourselves with others, deceptively causing us to be judgmental. We are often judgmental of others in order to exalt ourselves. In Luke 18:11, the Pharisee thanked God that he was not like other men: extortioners, unjust, adulterers or tax collectors. Such judging may take the form of gossip, slander or bitter

criticisms against church members. God instead asks us to forgive the failures of others (see, for example, Eph. 4:32; Col. 3:13). The religious spirit encourages judgment and unforgiveness because it knows that they can destroy the environment of God's love and peace within the Church.

- *The religious spirit will influence believers to be loveless, merciless and compassionless.* The religious spirit influences us to be loveless, merciless and compassionless by enticing us to focus on ourselves, ignoring the woes and pains of others. It will also induce us to be easily offended by others, causing us to respond in anger rather than love. Yet God calls us to be loving, merciful and compassionate; and if we move in the Spirit, we will be, for He gives us a spirit of love (see 2 Tim. 1:7).

- *The religious spirit will entice some to be prideful, self righteous and arrogant.* Pride, self-righteousness and arrogance cause us to focus on ourselves rather than on God. Focusing on God opens the way for the work of the Spirit. Focusing on self closes it. Prideful people come to believe that they don't need God or that they have a direct line to God and are never wrong. Others may develop a martyr mentality, thinking, *No one suffers like me.*

- *The religious spirit will cause believers to have negative attitudes about themselves.* When we have negative attitudes about ourselves, our focus is on our own plight and worthlessness and not on God's love and plan for provision and redemption. This is often accompanied by self-hatred and self-condemnation. Satan will lie to us that our transgressions are so deep that God cannot forgive them or redeem us. The Word says, however, that everything is possible with God and that He will forgive us and cleanse us of all unrighteousness (see Matt. 19:26; 1 John 1:9).

• *The religious spirit may implant a desire to be in control.* We may become afraid if we feel we are not in control. When *we* are in control, the Holy Spirit isn't; and the Word says that we are to be led by the Spirit (see Gal. 5:18). Being led by the Spirit means submitting all our decisions, both large and small, to the Lord.

Fostering Harmful Ideas and Attitudes

Having read this far into this chapter (and this book), you may be wondering whether the religious spirit has an inroad into your life. Here is a simple checklist that you can use to evaluate whether you have ideas and attitudes that separate you from God.

• *Do I see God as unloving, harsh and judgmental?* God is not unloving, harsh and judgmental. The truth is that "God so loved the world that He gave His only begotten Son" and "God is love" (John 3:16; 1 John 4:8).

• *Do I see God as distant and detached?* Distance and detachment stifle communion with God. A love relationship involves closeness and intimacy.

• *Do I think that I can't have fellowship with God or hear His voice?* Jesus said, "My sheep hear My voice, and I know them, and they follow Me" (John 10:27). Beware that the religious spirit may whisper a lie that we are not worthy of hearing God.

• *Do I have hardness of heart and dullness toward the things of God?* Jesus said that the Pharisees honored Him with their lips, but their hearts were far from him (see Matt.

15:8). When our hearts feel hard, let us kneel before Him and ask Him to soften them.

- *Do I hate spiritual correction?* Proverbs 3:11 instructs us, "Do not despise the chastening of the LORD." The Pharisees hated spiritual correction. They plotted to kill Jesus in response (see Matt. 26:4).

- *Do I avoid real repentance for sin through godly sorrow?* Sometimes when children are commanded to say that they are sorry, they pout and grudgingly say, "Sorry." We are called to express godly sorrow, which leads to repentance (see 2 Cor. 7:10). God will give us the gift of repentance when we ask Him for it.

- *Do I love the world and compromise with truth?* The Word of God says, "Do not love the world or the things in the world. If anyone loves the world, the love of the Father is not in him" (1 John 2:15). Whenever a Christian compromises with the world's system, whether it's with unsavory movies or television, coarse humor or sexual impropriety, it dilutes his or her witness, and the flow of God's blessing is weakened.

HOW TO DEAL WITH THE RELIGIOUS SPIRIT

The Bible says not to "give place to the devil" (Eph. 4:27). Demons can enter if they are given a place through sin. Sin puts us on common ground with the devil and gives him (and his demon spirits) a place from which to operate. "He who sins is of the devil, for the devil has sinned from the beginning" (1 John 3:8). Some ways that demons enter are through the embracing of false beliefs about God, unforgiveness, spiritual compromise, hypocrisy, fear, pride or inferiority. Generational sin can also provide a place of entry.

The good news is that the spirit of religion, like any other spirit, must yield to the power of God. Through years of deliverance ministry, we have seen many demons expelled in a moment, never to return. However, we have observed that the religious spirit often requires more time and ministry to cast out than some of the others, because it permeates so many facets of life and it has gained strength through years of its victims' yielding to its influence, usually without knowing they are being affected.

If you become concerned that you might be under the oppression of a religious spirit, you need to take action. In some cases, you yourself might be able to take authority and command it to leave. In other cases, however, you would be wise to seek out an experienced deliverance minister. Since Jesus, our deliverer, is the master strategist, it is important to inquire of Him which approach He chooses.

After you pray, you may be uncertain as to the presence of a religious spirit or your authority to cast out the spirit, or you may have no revelation as to what might have provided an opening for the spirit to enter. In any such case, the help of a mature and experienced member of the Body of Christ is invaluable. He or she needs to be gifted to receive revelation as to what might have provided an opening for the religious spirit to enter. After you close that door or doors and yield to the Holy Spirit, the religious spirit's grip will weaken. Then, in the name of Jesus, it can be commanded to leave.

When you seek deliverance from a religious spirit alone, begin by asking God to give you a revelation of how the religious spirit is manifesting. Since we want to be truly repentant for our sin of yielding to a religious spirit rather than God's Holy Spirit, asking Him to give us the gift of repentance and godly sorrow (see 2 Cor. 7:9-10) will help us to have God's heart and perspective concerning our cooperation with that spirit.

After you have repented in detail from your heart for the various ways you have obeyed the religious spirit, you may be led to take authority over the spirit and speak directly to it. Mark 16:17 says that we have authority in Jesus' name to cast out demon spirits. Acts 16:18 shows us that this is done by speaking directly to the spirit. Paul said to the spirit, "I command you in the name of Jesus Christ to come out of her." We therefore might say something like this:

You religious spirit, I have repented from yielding to you, and now I come against you in the name of Jesus. I forbid you to influence me. I take back all I have relinquished to you. I break your control over me, and I command you to release me in Jesus' name. Lord Jesus, fill me afresh with Your Holy Spirit. Help me be a person who walks in the Spirit and not under the control of a religious spirit. I ask You to dismantle every component of the false religious system in me.

It is important to note that we should not use this same prayer as a formula. The Holy Spirit must be the one leading the prayer time, or else our time of prayer becomes another manifestation of the religious spirit! And we must be sure that we are waging spiritual warfare under the power of the Holy Spirit and not from the flesh. So before you begin, call out to the Lord for an anointing of power, and move in faith, believing that God has anointed you. Actively adopt a posture of submission to the direction of the Holy Spirit. When you do so, you invite the power of the Holy Spirit to work against the enemy.

We know a man who loved God, but who was under the strong control of the religious spirit. We invited him for prayer. We asked the Lord for His anointing and that He would give this man revelation about the spirit's hold on him. Once the man received that revelation, he cried out for rescue. When we commanded the spirit to come out, the man shouted that his neck was paralyzed and that he could not move (much later we remembered Acts 7:51, where Stephen called the Jewish religious leaders "stiffnecked"). As we continued to come against the spirit, the man, who had been standing, suddenly emitted a loud sound and folded in half, his head almost touching the floor. When he stood up, we saw that his countenance had changed, and he had new freedom in the Holy Spirit. As time has passed since that day, he has come to know God more intimately, and he can receive God's love and give it to others more than ever before.

IN SUMMARY

Admittedly, the religious spirit is powerful and influential; but in the end, it is no match for God's passion to have an intimate relationship with each of us. God wants us to enjoy the freshness of a life permeated by the Holy Spirit. To that end, if we truly seek God for freedom, He will give us continued revelation of how the false religious system influences our lives, and He will give us power to dismantle the religious spirit's complex strategy. It is God's desire that the works and devices of that great imposter, the religious spirit, be vanquished and that we have freedom to know the true and living God and be led by the Holy Spirit to live out the plan and purpose of God for our lives.

ENDNOTES

Chapter One

1. Much of this material on the spirit of religion is also covered in chapter 1 of C. Peter Wagner, *Changing Church* (Ventura, CA: Regal Books, 2004).
2. The Second Apostolic Age, the New Apostolic Reformation and the changes associated with them are further explained in C. Peter Wagner, *The New Apostolic Churches* (Ventura, CA: Regal Books, 1998), *Churchquake!* (Ventura, CA: Regal Books, 1999) and *Changing Church* (Ventura, CA: Regal Books, 2004.
3. James Strong, *The New Strong's Exhaustive Concordance of the Bible* (Nashville, TN: Thomas Nelson Publishers, 1984), Hebrew ref. no. 1080.

Chapter Four

1. James Strong, *The New Strong's Exhaustive Concordance of the Bible* (Nashville, TN: Thomas Nelson Publishers, 1984), Greek ref. no. 2215.

Chapter Five

1. James Strong, *The New Strong's Exhaustive Concordance of the Bible* (Nashville, TN: Thomas Nelson Publishers, 1984), Greek ref. no. 2962.
2. Strong, *The New Strong's Exhaustive Concordance of the Bible,* Greek ref. no. 863.
3. Joseph Henry Thayer, *A Greek-English Lexicon of the New Testament* (Grand Rapids, MI: Baker Book House, 1977), Strong's Greek ref. no. 3845.
4. Colin Brown, ed., *The New International Dictionary of New Testament Theology,* vol. 2 (Grand Rapids, MI: Regency Reference Library, 1986), pp. 467-468.
5. Following the apostle Paul's example, I call the spirit of religion a spirit of stupor, instead of calling it a spirit of deep sleep. In Romans 11:8 Paul quoted from Isaiah 29:10 and translated the phrase "a spirit of deep sleep" as "a spirit of stupor."
6. C. F. Keil and F. Delitzsch, *Commentary on the Old Testament: Isaiah 28—66,* 3rd ed., trans. James Martin (Peabody, MA: Hendrickson Publishers), p. 22.
7. Strong, *The New Strong's Exhaustive Concordance of the Bible,* Hebrew ref. no. 8639.
8. Keil and Delitzsch, *Commentary on the Old Testament: Isaiah 28—66,* p. 21.
9. Ernst Kasemann, *Commentary on Romans,* 4th ed. (Grand Rapids, MI: Wm. B. Eerdmans Publishing Co., 1980), p. 302.

10. Albert Barnes, *Notes on the New Testament: Romans* (Grand Rapids, MI: Baker Book House, 1949), p. 248.
11. Ernst Kasemann, *Commentary on Romans*, p. 302.
12. A. T. Robertson, *Word Pictures in the New Testament*, vol. 4 (Grand Rapids, MI: Baker Book House, 1931), p. 393.
13. Barnes, *Notes on the New Testament: Romans*, p. 247.

Chapter Six

1. *Webster's Talking Dictionary/Thesaurus*, CD-ROM, version 1.0b (Exceller Software Corporation).

Chapter Seven

1. James Strong, *The New Strong's Exhaustive Concordance of the Bible* (Nashville, TN: Thomas Nelson Publishers, 1984), Greek ref. no. 2513.
2. Joseph Henry Thayer, *A Greek-English Lexicon of the New Testament* (Grand Rapids, MI: Baker Book House, 1977), Strong's Greek ref. no. 5331.
3. Strong, *The New Strong's Exhaustive Concordance of the Bible*, Hebrew ref. no. 5391.
4. Ibid., Greek ref. no. 3446.
5. Ibid., Greek ref. no. 3445.
6. Thayer, *A Greek-English Lexicon of the New Testament*, Strong's Greek ref. no. 2965.
7. Strong, *The New Strong's Exhaustive Concordance of the Bible*, Greek ref. no. 945.
8. *Merriam-Webster's Collegiate Dictionary*, 11th ed., s.v. "fruit."
9. Strong, *The New Strong's Exhaustive Concordance of the Bible*, Hebrew ref. no. 1892.
10. Ibid., Hebrew ref. no. 1891.

Leila